SUTTON POCKET HISTORIES

CHARTISM

ASA BRIGGS

SUTTON PUBLISHING

First published in the United Kingdom in 1998 by
Sutton Publishing Limited · Phoenix Mill
Thrupp · Stroud · Gloucestershire · GL5 2BU

British Library Cataloguing in Publication Data
A catalogue record for this book is available from the British
Library.

ISBN 0-7509-1916-7

Cover illustration: Detail from *Procession attending the Great National
petition, 1842*, from a contemporary engraving (National
Museum of Labour History).

 ™ ALAN SUTTON™ and SUTTON™ are the
trade marks of Sutton Publishing Limited

Typeset in 11/16 pt Baskerville.
Typesetting and origination by
Sutton Publishing Limited.
Printed in Great Britain by
The Guernsey Press Company Limited
Guernsey, Channel Islands.

*Dedicated
to all the historians
of Chartism
Past, Present and Future*

'Who knew anything of the history of the working classes? Some books had been published with some pretensions of the kind; but they really contained nothing at all to the purpose; and he should not be surprised if a good history of the working classes should one day be published by one of themselves, and which would really deserve its title.'

(The Northern Star report of a speech by John Collins at a Chartist rally in Manchester, welcoming him and Peter Murray M'Douall after their release from gaol, 22 August 1840)

'It is extremely unlikely that any competent or satisfactory narrative of a stupendous national crisis [Chartism] will ever now be given to the world.'

(W.E. Adams, Memoirs of a Social Atom, 1903)

Contents

Acknowledgements

I am deeply grateful to Susan Hard and to Pat Spencer for their invaluable help in preparing this Pocket History for publication. I am grateful too to the London Library and over the years to archivists and librarians in many different parts of the country without whose willing cooperation such a book would be impossible. I owe much to the many students, undergraduate and postgraduate, who have explored Chartism with me. I am entirely responsible, however, for the contents and style of *Chartism*. The subject has always interested me deeply as a professional historian.

Lewes
May 1998

List of Dates

LIST OF DATES

1829   **June**. Creation of Peel's Metropolitan Police.
December. The Birmingham Political Union of the Lower and Middle Classes of the People (BPU) formed.

1830   **June**. Death of George IV.
November. Return of the Whigs to power under Earl Grey.

1831   **March**. The Reform Bill introduced by Lord John Russell.
April. Richard Oastler's *Manifesto to the Working Classes of the West Riding* demanding a statutory ten-hour working day.
May. The National Union of the Working Classes founded in London.
Ebenezer Elliott publishes *Corn Law Rhymes*.

1832   **June**. The Reform Bill becomes law.
December. First general election under the new electoral system.

1833   **May**. Irish Coercion Act.
August. Passing of Althorp's Factory Act limiting children's working day. Inspectors to check.

1834   **January**. Formation of Robert Owen's Grand National Consolidated Trades Union (collapses October).
March. Six Dorchester labourers, the 'Tolpuddle Martyrs', sentenced to transportation.
April. Great London demonstration in support of Dorchester labourers.
July. Poor Law Amendment Act.

1835   'Lichfield House Compact' between Daniel O'Connell and Whigs: final split between O'Connell and Feargus O'Connor.

1836   **March**. Reduction of newspaper stamp duty to 1*d* per issue.

June. London Working Men's Association (LWMA) founded by William Lovett (and others).

1837   **January**. East London Democratic Association formed. The Poor Law Commissioners turn their attention to the industrial districts.

28 February. Meeting of Radicals called by LWMA at the Crown and Anchor Tavern in the Strand – adoption of a Reform Petition.

March. Birmingham petitions on industrial distress.

April. Glasgow cotton spinners strike.

May. BPU revived.

June. Conference between LWMA and MPs about further Parliamentary reform.

BPU decides to petition Parliament demanding universal suffrage and currency reform.

July. General election: defeat of many Radical MPs.

November. Rebellions in Upper and Lower Canada.

7 November. BPU decides to concentrate on universal suffrage.

18 November. First issue of *The Northern Star* in Leeds.

December. Prosecution of leaders of the Glasgow Cotton Spinners' Union: found guilty and sentenced to seven years' transportation.

Government at O'Connell's suggestion sets up an official inquiry into trade unions. The trade unions set up their own committee, including three LMWA representatives.

1838   **8 May**. People's Charter published in London.

1838   **21 May**. Mass meeting in Glasgow: speakers from LWMA, BPU and Glasgow Cotton Spinners.

5 June. O'Connor establishes Great Northern Union.

27 June. Mass meeting on Town Moor, Newcastle-upon-Tyne: Northern Political Union founded.

1 August. Mass meeting on Newhall Hill, Birmingham.

Summer and autumn. Election of members to the General Convention.

17 September. Meeting at Palace Yard, Westminster, to elect London members.

24 September. Huge mass demonstration on Kersal Moor, Manchester, presided over by John Fielden.

September. Founding of Manchester Anti-Corn Law Association.

Autumn. Torchlight meetings in Lancashire.

14 November. J.R. Stephens's address at an open air Lancashire meeting leads to his arrest.

8 December. Mass meeting at Calton Hill, Edinburgh.

1839   **January**. Committal to trial of Stephens.

4 February. Opening of Convention of the Industrious Classes.

April. Maj-Gen Sir Charles Napier is approached to command Northern District of the Army.

February. John Frost removed by Home Secretary from the Commission of the Peace.

March. Anti-Corn Law League set up as a national organisation.

April–May. Riots at Llanidloes, Wales.

7 May. Petition given to Thomas Attwood and Fielden to present to Parliament.

1839   **11 May**. Melbourne asks for Parliament to be dissolved.
13 May. Convention moves to Birmingham.
Consideration of 'ulterior measures'.
Whitsuntide. Mass demonstrations.
1 July. Convention reconvenes in Birmingham.
4 July. Bull Ring riots in Birmingham.
6 July. Lovett and Collins arrested and committed to
Warwick Gaol.
12 July. Attwood and Fielden present Petition to
Parliament calling for Committee of the Whole House
to examine it. Rejected (235 to 46).
Convention returns to London.
15 July. Convention calls for the 'Three-Day Holiday' to
begin on 12 August.
Further disturbances in Birmingham.
July–August. Rural Police Bill debated and passed.
Bank rate raised to 5 per cent.
6 August. Resolution calling off the Sacred Month.
'Three-Day Holiday' proposed.
Summer. Many Chartist arrests.
6 September. Convention dissolves.
5 October–2 November. O'Connor in Ireland.
3 November. March of Welsh Chartists on Newport.
4 November. Attack on Westgate Hotel.
The Newport Rising.
O'Connor creates Defence Fund.
10 December. Special Commission at Monmouth to
frame charges against Welsh Chartist leaders.
31 December. Trial of John Frost begins.

1840   Winter and spring. Many Chartist arrests and trials.

1840 **9 January**. 'Guilty' verdict on Frost.
Abortive risings in Sheffield and Bradford, followed by arrests.
Arrest of armed Chartists in Bethnal Green.
12 January. Abortive rising at Dewsbury.
Abortive Sheffield rising. Imprisonment of Samuel Holberry who dies in gaol (21 June).
13 January. Sentence to death of Frost and leaders of Newport Rising.
26 January. Abortive rising at Bradford.
1 February. Newport leaders' sentences commuted to transportation.
April. Northern Political Union reorganised in Newcastle-upon-Tyne.
May. Leeds Parliamentary Reform Association.
20 July. Delegate meeting at Manchester sets up National Charter Association (NCA).
24 July. Lovett and Collins are released from Warwick Gaol.
Attempts to create Chartist-Radical Association in Leeds. Other releases and home comings.

1841 **April**. Lovett founds the National Association of the United Kingdom for Promoting the Political and Social Improvement of the People.
O'Connor takes up the land question as a 'remedy for national poverty'.
August. General election. Conservative victory. Peel becomes Prime Minister.
November. Joseph Sturge takes up the suffrage issue and founds the Complete Suffrage Union.

1842   **April**. Complete Suffrage Union Conference at Birmingham.

Chartist Convention in London.

May. Commons rejects the second Petition (287 to 49).

July. Trough of the trade cycle: wage cuts, unemployment.

August–September. The 'Plug Riots'.

December. Conference of the Chartist and Complete Suffrage representatives in Birmingham. Collapse of the CSU.

1843   **March**. Trial and acquittal on main points of O'Connor and other Chartists.

September. Chartist Convention in Birmingham: Land Plan accepted. The Chartist Executive moves to London.

1844   **April**. Chartist Convention at Manchester.

August. Debate between O'Connor and Cobden at Northampton.

November. Title of *The Northern Star* changed to *Northern Star and National Trades Journal*: headquarters moved from Leeds to London.

December. The 'Rochdale Pioneers' open their Toad Lane cooperative store.

1845   **April**. Chartist convention in London: the Chartist Land Co-operative Society launched.

May. Rules of the Land Society published.

September. Society of Fraternal Democrats founded by George Julian Harney.

December. Manchester Conference on the Land Plan

1846   **June**. Repeal of the Corn Laws. Split in Peel's Conservative Party.

December. Birmingham Conference on the Land Plan.

1847   **April**. National financial crisis.
        May. Ten Hours Factory Act passed.
        O'Connorville is opened.
        July. General election. Whig victory. Lord John Russell
        became Prime Minister. O'Connor elected at
        Nottingham. Harney opposes Palmerston at Tiverton,
        Ernest Jones contests Halifax.
        August. Lowbands Conference on the Land Plan.
        Autumn and winter. Mounting unemployment:
        collection of signatures for third Chartist Petition.

1848   **February**. Revolution in France.
        Publication of the *Communist Manifesto*.
        10 April. Chartist Convention summoned in London.
        Kennington Common demonstration.
        13 April. Third National Petition laughed out by the
        House of Commons (no division).
        Joseph Hume's 'Little Charter' movement takes shape.
        May. Chartist National Assembly summoned.
        Select Committee of the House of Commons appointed
        to investigate the Land Plan.
        May–July. Provincial Chartist disturbances: large-scale
        arrests; imprisonment of Jones and others.
        30 July. Publication of the Select Committee's
        Reports.

1849   **March**. The National Parliamentary and Financial
        Reform Association founded.
        22 May (eve of Derby Day). Hume's Little Charter.
        June. Parliamentary reform motion, supported by Hume
        and O'Connor, defeated in the House of Commons
        (286 to 82).

ONE

Perspectives

The history of Chartism, the greatest movement of popular protest in British history, has been told and retold many times and in many different ways, and there is no definitive version. The first histories were written by old Chartists: they had an autobiographical dimension, and the accounts set out in them and the assessment of the characters involved did not converge. The first of them, *A History of the Chartist Movement*, by R.G. Gammage, was published in 1854: Thomas Wheeler's *A Brief Life of Feargus O'Connor* appeared a year later. No two sets of assessments could have been more different. The first damned O'Connor'; the second praised him.

During the last decades of the nineteenth century, when the British labour movement was developing on quite different lines, culminating in the foundation of the Labour Party, most stress was placed for politically relevant reasons not on structural differences but on historical continuity, with 'the Chartist struggle' being related to other popular struggles, old and new.

Thus, Benjamin Wilson, writing his reminiscences, *The Struggle of an Old Chartist and the Part he has taken in Various Movements*, in the *Halifax Courier* in 1887 looked back to times before his own birth when he summed up what Chartists had sought to achieve as 'a voice in making the laws they were called upon to obey': the most basic of their Six Points was universal suffrage. 'They believed [as the Americans had done] that taxation without representation was tyranny and right to be resisted'. This political aspect of Chartism deserves emphasis. The Chartists were conscious both of their power and of their powerlessness. Wilson, who was introduced to Chartism by his aunt, whom he described as 'a famous politician, a Chartist and a great admirer of Feargus O'Connor', went on to describe the context of power in the early decades of the nineteenth century when he added that the Chartists:

took a leading part in agitating in favour of the ten hours
question [restricting by law the length of the factory working
day], the repeal of the taxes on knowledge [newspaper
duties], education, cooperation, civil and religious liberty
and the land question, for they were the true pioneers of all
the great movements of their time.

Significantly the repeal of the Corn Laws did not
figure on this list.

One of the first accounts of Chartism written by a
non-participant of a different generation, who came
from a very different social background from
Wilson's, was that by the political scientist Graham
Wallas (b. 1858), who liked to describe himself as a
'working thinker'. His lectures to the Fabian Society
on Chartism, delivered in 1888, one year after
Wilson's reminiscences appeared, persuaded George
Bernard Shaw of 'the necessity for mastering the
history of our own movement and falling into our
ordered place in it'.

Wallas also wrote *The Life of Francis Place* (1898),
drawing uncritically on the voluminous Place Papers
then kept in the British Museum. Interested in
everything that was happening in radical politics,

Place, famous as 'the radical tailor of Charing Cross', retained everything he thought should be preserved about radicalism, including much that would have been regarded by his contemporaries as ephemera. He was at times an active participant in politics as well as an observer, and in both capacities he was a judge of motives as well as of movements. He was sixty-five years old when he helped to draft the Charter, and he himself has to be judged as critically as he judged others.

The first English professional historian to deal with Chartism, Mark Hovell, depended on Place. His carefully researched but unfinished book, *The Chartist Movement* (1918), was based on talks to Workers' Educational Association (WEA) classes: so, too, was a pamphlet on Chartism (1929) by Hugh Gaitskell, a future leader of the Labour Party. Hovell, like Place, disparages O'Connor, as does the great Manchester University medieval scholar T.F. Tout, who finished the book for Hovell and who showed the manuscript to Wallas and to Julius West, a Russian exile and a clerk in the Fabian Society's office. West also died before his own *History of Chartism* could be published in 1920. His book was finished by the literary pundit J.C. Squire, whose qualifications to finish it were less than those of Tout.

Hovell's account, supplemented by G.D.H. Cole's *Chartist Portraits*, published during the Second World War in 1940 – with the great economic depression of the interwar years between – remained the standard text until a new generation of scholars, many from provincial working-class backgrounds, some of them women, took up the subject again in the 1950s. This was after the post-war Labour Government, with a huge majority, had carried through a large number of legislative measures that were conceived of as a further, if not final, episode in the story of the 'victory of the vanquished'. They were part of a 'great march' across time. Labour had been defeated, however, at the general election of 1951, and it now seemed particularly relevant not just to describe the fate of Chartism but to explain it.

Professional historians now began to pay attention to the diverse 'roots' of Chartism in the different 'localities', a term used by the Chartists, and to its geography, with *Chartist Studies* (1959) providing a stimulus to detailed local research. The extent of their success was substantial. Chartism acquired new depth. This was history from below.

There have been many subsequent layers of historical interpretation of Chartism; and as it has been studied at many different levels – local, regional and national – so it has been related not only to the Labour Party, which had to wait for more than half a century before coming into existence, but also to the Gladstonian Liberal Party, which emerged within twenty years of the Chartist eclipse.

This is a British story, but Chartist history has always had an international dimension too. Foreigners from Karl Marx and Friedrich Engels onwards – and they were contemporary observers (and judges) of what was happening – have been just as fascinated by the movement as Britons. Edouard Dolléans published two volumes, *Le Chartisme* (1912–13), never translated from French into English: it had a preface by Sidney Webb and related Chartism directly to industrialisation as Marx and Engels did at the time. Dolléans's book was never read by Hovell, who was killed in action in France one year before the Bolshevik

Revolution, but he had read Max Beer's two-volume *Geschichte des Sozialismus in England*, which appeared in 1913 and which was translated from the German as the *History of British Socialism* after the end of the war.

It was Beer who memorably described the fate of Chartism as 'the victory of the vanquished'. As he pointed out, each of the Chartists' Six Points, except annual parliaments, had been achieved. Universal suffrage had begun to include women as well as men, as many of the Chartists had wanted when the Charter was drafted.

This story was interesting to Americans also, and two books on Chartism appeared in the United States during the First World War before Lenin, echoing Engels, described Chartism as the world's 'first broad and politically organised proletarian-revolutionary movement of the masses'.

Before and after the collapse of the Soviet Union two centuries after the French Revolution other generations of scholars (including research students in universities) have extended and in some cases revised the Chartist story without any of them telling it in full. They have tended to take sides, driven sometimes by ideology, always by temperament, usually by the intensity and depth of their research. All of them have been influenced by E.P. Thompson who related 'the making of an English working class' conscious of its identity not only to industrialisation but to an indigenous and distinctive radical tradition which looked back as far as the Anglo-Saxons and which was renewed and reshaped in the eighteenth century.

The making of Chartism out of a diversity of ingredients is as interesting as its subsequent history as a national movement. O'Connor, the Irish-born Chartist leader, has been rehabilitated by more than one historian, notably by James Epstein in his lively book *The Lion of Freedom* (1982); Epstein quotes approvingly O'Connor's proud claim that he was a 'demagogue'. William Lovett, founder of the London Working Men's Association (LWMA), who was praised by Hovell, has been played down by Epstein and by others, yet he never has been – nor can be – kept out of the story. Nor can Bronterre O'Brien, 'the Schoolmaster of Chartism', eleven years younger than fellow Irishman O'Connor and for many years his close ally, for he was a shrewd analyst of issues and tactics.

The importance of relationships, personal and political, between the three Irishmen O'Connor, O'Brien and O'Connell is now fully appreciated, particularly the relationship between O'Connor and O'Connell, 'the Liberator'. The latter dominated the Irish (and a significant part of the English) political scene in 1833 when O'Connor was elected Member of Parliament for County Cork. It has become clear just how integrally the history of Ireland is bound up with the history of Chartism, particularly at the beginning and at the end of the story. O'Connell, a supporter of the New Poor Law, was willing to work with and through the Whigs at Westminster, while retaining massive Irish support in England as well as Ireland.

In most twentieth-century discussions of Chartism narrative has never been separated from analysis, and the analysis has pivoted on the nature of political leadership, on the interrelationship of political and economic factors, although the latter are no longer treated as basic by many historians, and on the sense of class consciousness. Most recently there has been a switch of interest to the language that Chartists employed, verbal (not just the language of class) and non-verbal, within what has been conceived of as a distinctive Chartist culture. Yet in my view the economics can never be left out. Chartism was described at the time as a 'knife and fork' or a 'bread and cheese' question – and there was more talk of 'roast beef' than of equal electoral districts. The economic fortunes of employers and employed, determined by fluctuations in industry and trade, then directly related to the state of harvest, remain an essential part of the background of Chartism and any assessment of its 'successes' and 'failures'.

There were 'good' and 'bad' years, and, while disparaged by some recent historians, the kind of 'social tension chart' prepared in 1948 by the American historian W.W. Rostow that lists these years remains useful. So, too, does Robin Matthews's detailed study of economic fluctuations between 1833 and 1842. There were, of course, highly relevant structural as well as cyclical economic factors. The pull of early Chartism was particularly strong in old centres of decaying or contracting industry, like

Trowbridge in Wiltshire, or Carmarthen in Wales, or in new and expanding single-industry towns like cotton-producing Stockport, described by Engels as 'one of the darkest and smokiest holes' in the cotton textile district of Lancashire. Another smaller Lancashire town, Ashton, has been described as 'the most Chartist locality' in Britain.

Yet while the extent of the appeal of Chartism was strongly influenced by economic factors and there were many 'foul weather' Chartists who abandoned the movement in 'good times', it was more than an expression of distress. Poverty was endemic and rights were judged eternal. Articulate Chartists had their own versions of political economy, which also related to all times and all places. Labour was the source of all value and 'the labourers ought to possess the earth'. 'Your share in law-making would ensure for you a share in the distribution of the wealth which you create'. O'Brien put it all very simply: 'Knaves will tell you that it is because you have no property that you are unrepresented. I tell you on the contrary that it is because you are unrepresented that you have no property.' Cooperation, not competition which many Chartists judged 'unnatural', should be the basis of an economy that would serve the needs of labour and in the long run the interests of all.

The economy would be less dependent – some Chartists said not at all dependent – on foreign trade, and this conclusion helps to explain, but does not completely explain, the emphasis on the land in Chartist political economy. While Chartism was not strong – in some cases it was almost non-existent, for example in completely agricultural villages like those of Kent or in old market towns like Ripon or Bedford – many industrial workers, some of them first generation recruits to the factories, wished to 'return to the land'.

Psychology was as relevant in this connection as political economy, making a 'land plan' central to Chartism, not peripheral to it. There were divisions between O'Connor and O'Brien and others on what a land plan should incorporate and these were at least as important as those divisions on which many history textbooks have concentrated, particularly the issue, temperamental and tactical, of 'moral' versus 'physical force', an issue that can be easily simplified. Even Chartists who were repelled by the language of physical force believed in the slogan 'Peacefully if we may, forcibly if we must'.

In many textbooks the story of Chartism is told briefly. It began with the publication in London of the People's Charter in May 1838 and ended, also in London, after the last of the three unsuccessful petitions to Parliament in April 1848, a year of European revolutions, with the word 'fiasco' being often used to describe the events of 10 April 1848. This was a day that even in the briefest of histories is given as much attention as that given to most years: seeking to process from Kennington Common to Westminster to deliver the final Chartist petition, which was said to have 5,700,000 signatories, the Chartists, led by O'Connor and far fewer in numbers than they had threatened or expected, dispersed quietly south of the River Thames. This was after the Commissioner of Police, Richard Mayne, had told O'Connor that the procession had been declared illegal and that he had authority from the Whig government to meet the procession with force if it tried to reach the House of Commons. O'Connor, at that time a Member of Parliament for Nottingham, yielded, and only four cabs, the last of them bearing himself, were allowed to cross Westminster Bridge. Parliament referred the Petition to a Committee, which reported that there were large numbers of forgeries among the less than two million signatures: they included (seventeen times) that of the Duke of Wellington, who was in charge of the government's forces in the capital on 10 April, and that of 'Victoria Rex [not Regina], 1 April'.

Such summary accounts of a movement without precedent in the scale of its organisation usually also involve a comparison between the success of the 'middle-class' Anti-Corn Law League, founded in March 1839, which concentrated on repeal of the Corn Laws as its single objective and secured it in 1846 (a year of famine in Ireland), and the failure of the 'working-class' Chartist movement, which was not only torn by divisions but was badly led. In such accounts, which overestimate the political role of the League and the 'unity' of the middle classes, tribute is usually paid to the political skills of

Richard Cobden, its main leader, who is favourably compared with O'Connor. The 'aftermath' of 10 April 1848, which was by no means the last day in Chartist history, is dealt with very briefly, although it is noted that O'Connor, after being involved in personal, not group, disturbances in and out of Parliament in 1852, was declared insane and removed to a Chiswick asylum. He died in August 1855.

During their own time the Chartists secured none of the Six Points set out in their Charter – in 1848 they had been reduced to five – although five of them were to be implemented at various dates in the future in very different circumstances. Ironically, the one Point omitted in 1848, the Ballot, which had not figured on the original working-class agenda, was the first to be introduced (by a Liberal government) in 1872. There was no irony in the fact that in February 1838, before the Charter was drafted, no fewer than 198 Members of Parliament voted in favour of the Ballot – with 315 against. For most articulate Chartists the Ballot was useless – or even dangerous – without universal suffrage. It was exclusion from political power that was the cause of 'social anomalies' (Gammage's words).

Political power could – and would – remedy them, a deduction challenged by most Whigs, not least the Whig historian T.B. Macaulay, not writing in a history book but speaking against the Charter in Parliament in 1842 when the second National Petition was presented. For him universal suffrage would be 'fatal to all purposes for which Government exists'.

The relationship of Parliamentary radicals – not an organised party – to Whigs between 1830 and 1841 requires more attention than is usually given to them both in long and short accounts of Chartism. So, too, do the attitudes and policies of Sir Robert Peel, Conservative Prime Minister from 1841 to 1847, the statesman who removed some of the economic causes of discontent.

After the Conservative Party split on the issue of Corn Law repeal in 1846 – as important a political date in British history as 1832 – and after the death of Peel in 1850 'Peelites', including Gladstone, were to join with many ex-Chartists, men like Robert

Lowery, in the creation of a new Liberal Party that had a popular base. The word 'Chartism' did not appear in any of the standard histories of Liberalism. It did appear, however, in 1876 in the ninth edition of the *Encyclopaedia Britannica*, which ended its brief account:

> The return of national prosperity relieved the working classes of the most pressing grievances, and subsequent legislative changes have in great measure relieved the causes that existed for discontent among the classes which most supported the Charter.

'Chartism' has always figured, of course, in standard histories of socialism, a movement that gained in strength after the ninth edition of the *Encyclopaedia* appeared; and within this context the spotlight has sometimes been placed less on O'Connor, who was never a socialist, than on two other figures, the first of them an unlikely character to be found in the *dramatis personae* either of Chartism or of socialism. Ernest Jones, son of a soldier and equerry (and godson of the Duke of Cumberland, one of Queen Victoria's 'wicked uncles', who became King of Hanover in 1837), played no part in Chartism in its early years, but his subsequent political career (praised by Hovell) led through from 1848 to the Manchester general election of 1868, when he was a Liberal candidate: this was in the first election to follow the next extension of the suffrage in the Reform Act of 1867. George Julian Harney, the second figure, played an interesting role in Chartism from the start; he modelled himself on the French revolutionary Marat, and in the late 1840s he was in regular contact with Marx and Engels. His substantial library was stocked with volumes on the French Revolution.

After 1848 when Chartism had ceased to be a mass movement, both Jones and Harney were to demand 'the Charter and Something More', a 'Something More' that included land nationalisation, a 'land plan' very different from that which O'Connor and his supporters had fought for during the 1840s. It also included labour laws that would free workers from 'industrial slavery' (there was a link here with the Ten Hours movement); the reform of the Poor Law (further discredited in 1848 by recent scandals in administration) and provision for the support of 'the unemployed until labour is provided'; the disestablishment of the Church of England; a system of universal free education, including industrial schools that would supersede the apprenticeship system; and last, but not the least interesting, the encouragement through state aid of 'cooperative endeavour'. In the twilight years of Chartism we listen to different voices from those of 1838 or 1848, but as far as the last demand is concerned we return in a circle to the British Association for Promoting Cooperative Knowledge of 1829, a body to which Lovett belonged. In examining the demands as a whole we anticipate late twentieth-century 'welfare politics'.

Looking neither backwards nor forwards, some of the best recent writing on Chartism, focusing more on the Chartist rank and file than on the Chartist leadership, has been less concerned with placing the movement in short-term or long-term perspective than in evaluating what has been called 'the Chartist experience'. There has been a quest for immediacy and this has meant recapturing lost ways of thinking and feeling about politics and society. This in turn has demanded a sympathetic study of the language Chartists used to express not only their experiences at work and in the community but also their hopes and fears in a society that did not treat them as equals – a language not just of words but of symbols too, including flags and banners. The ballads and the hymns (and there was no shortage of either) are an essential part of the evidence too. Gammage called them 'gaudy trappings'.

Valuable and refreshing though such a new approach to Chartism is, it is less a substitute for gaining perspective than a necessary step towards acquiring it. Historically the Chartist movement, as in its own time, must be considered in terms of culmination as much as of legacy; and just how it was brought into existence throws light on group politics before and after the Chartist protest as much as on individual psychology. Chartism was Britain's last great platform agitation, and O'Connor can be compared more profitably with 'Orator' Henry Hunt (as John Belchem has done) than with Richard Cobden. Chartist speeches, pithy or verbose, usually the latter though there were some catchy slogans, should never be separated completely from their context. J.L. and Barbara Hammond wrote a lively and once widely read book called *The Age of the Chartists, 1832 to 1852* (1930) that had less to say of Chartism and of the Chartists than of other aspects of the society from which it emerged, and these other aspects must always be taken into account in considering both the Chartist experience and the Chartist story.

In placing Chartism within the context of a divided society any convincing synthesis must deal with the history both of 'working classes' and 'middle classes' (because of their heterogeneity in each case a plural is necessary) and not just with Chartists. Within such a context it is clear now, as it was at the time, that on 10 April 1848 it was 'the middle classes' – a term requiring as much scrutiny as the terms 'working classes', 'proletariat', 'bourgeoisie' or, indeed, 'the People' – who proved *their* strength. Moreover, their strength still had to be related to the continuing strength of the aristocracy to whom some middle-class leaders, notably Cobden, were bitterly and irrevocably opposed. The word 'democracy' was seldom employed.

When the day was over, the Chartists returned to their homes 'angry, hungry, footsore', while the Special Constables reinforcing the Duke of Wellington's carefully concealed troops could find ample comfort in the triumph of law and order. There were 8,000 troops and the Special Constables included Gladstone and the future Napoleon III. Lord John Russell, the Home Secretary and a central character in the story, protected the Home Office with huge piles of Blue Books. No one was killed. No one was seriously injured. It was possible, therefore, for Lady Palmerston, the wife of the Foreign Secretary, who himself commanded a garrison in Downing Street, to conclude that it was 'fortunate that the whole thing [had] occur'd, as it has shown the good spirit of our middle classes, and almost one may say of the whole population of London, as well as the activity and courage of the aristocracy'. It would, Lady Palmerston believed, 'have a great effect everywhere, in England, in Ireland [then an island of revolutionary discontent] and in Europe'.

This, too, was the belief of the young Queen Victoria, who came to the throne in 1837, the year when Chartism was in the crucible, and who was to give her name to an age that near its end was to see the foundation of the Labour Party. Born in the year of Peterloo, she was to find confirmation of her confidence in the working classes in their response to the Great Exhibition held in the Crystal Palace; her husband, Prince Albert, designed 'labourers' cottages' for it. In 1848 he had asked the government to do 'what it could to help the working classes over the present distress'.

Lady Palmerston's words should not be the last words in evaluating 1848. The conclusion to this Pocket History is the same as that reached in a comparison of O'Connor and O'Brien. I made it, appropriately in Ireland, in 1968:

> It is difficult to see how, given the nature of English society and government in the Chartist period, the Chartists could have succeeded in the way that O'Connor's critics claim that they might have done. The cards were too heavily stacked against them.

It was the strength of many of the Chartists that they did not abandon hope of reform, even of regeneration, in 1848 or in 1851. When Lovett was asked in September 1848 – after Kennington Common – what had led to his change of views as a Chartist – and by then he was off the stage – he replied simply that he was still 'as sincere a Chartist as I ever was, though I have generally differed from the bulk of my Chartist brethren regarding the best mode of securing the legal enactment of the People's Charter'. He had faith to believe, he added, 'that at no distant period the principles of the People's Charter will be the law of England'. It was all a question of time.

TWO

The Charter

Time past counts as well as time to come. Memory shapes vision. There was nothing new about the Six Points of the Charter, which was published in London on 8 May 1838. Nor was there anything new, except the scale, in the pattern of agitation that followed its publication. Many of the people involved in the early stages of the Chartist movement were political veterans. They invoked the names of Paine and Cobbett, and in the north of Henry Hunt. There were lines of descent.

Lovett, then thirty-eight years old, looked to Robert Owen, who was still alive, the creator of the most recent tradition; his autobiography, *The Life and Struggles of William Lovett* (1876), is essential reading. A self-taught craftsman, who helped to draft the Charter, Lovett had been associated in 1828 with

the First London Cooperative Trading Association,
seeking to put Owen's principles into practice.
O'Connor, four years older, was another veteran. He
took no part in drafting the Charter – and left
behind him no autobiography – but he always made
clear his debt to the line of Irish radical descent to
which he belonged. His political skill lay in the fact
that he could appeal also to the discontented in the
north of England and in parts of Scotland,
recognising that their lines of descent were different
from his own. He knew well how to challenge
authority: he could make it sound stupid as well as
wicked.

Unlike some of his supporters in the north,
O'Connor immediately appreciated the political
value of the Charter as a common platform.
Moreover, he could make use of his newspaper, *The
Northern Star*, to circulate the message widely,
providing a 'mental link . . . which . . . for the first
time concentrated the national mood into one
body'. The Charter was good news. The name
Northern Star itself carried echoes from his family
past: it had been the title in 1792 of a newspaper

published by the Belfast Committee of the United Irishmen, a political group to which his father and his uncle, later banished, both belonged.

There were more than echoes in Yorkshire. The publisher of the new *Northern Star*, Joshua Hobson, had edited the unstamped *Voice of the West Riding* from 1833 to 1835, a newspaper that recorded the fierce struggles of the factory reformers seeking to shorten the working day and of the opponents of the Whigs' Poor Law Amendment of 1834. O'Connor was prepared to pay the stamp duty on the new *Northern Star*, describing the 'little red stamp' as 'the Whig beauty spot, your plague spot'.

In all parts of the country a battle during the 1830s for a 'Cheap and Honest Press', free from fiscal duties (paper was taxed too) served as the prelude to Chartism, with Lovett helping to organise an educative campaign in London in the interests of the unstamped 'Pauper Press'. When in March 1836 the Whigs reduced stamp duty to 1*d*, splitting middle-class from working-class radicals, the popular struggle for full Press freedom was one of the national issues (it could not be called sectional) that was 'swallowed up' in Chartism. For O'Brien 'the rich man's paper had been made cheaper, the poor man's dearer.' A direct connection came through him: he had edited at its peak the unstamped *Poor Man's Guardian*, organ of the National Union of the Working Classes, launched in December 1830 by Lovett's friend and colleague Henry Hetherington. When he started writing for the *Star*, Richard Oastler, leader of the campaign for a statutory limitation of factory hours, asked him to take 'the soul' of the old paper with him.

Before the Charter was drafted, the pioneers of the 'Pauper Press', who included Hetherington, Yorkshireman James Watson and Irishman John Cleave, who published the *Weekly Police Gazette*, were already accustomed to 'struggle' and to imprisonment in consequence of their part in it. Hetherington was imprisoned three times, as was Watson (in 1833 for selling the *Poor Man's Guardian*). Cleave was imprisoned twice. To have been imprisoned became a Chartist qualification, although prison itself was never idealised. 'Feargus O'Connor herding and feeding with convicted felons' ran an editorial in *The Northern Star* when their leader was imprisoned in York Castle from May 1840 to August 1841.

The provincial salesmen of radical unstamped papers were as much Chartists in the making as their editors and publishers. For all of them the word 'struggle' was at the core of their vocabulary. They applied it both to individual lives, as in Lovett's autobiography, and to class relationships, with the word 'class' (seldom used in the Marxist sense) being given a greater place in political discourse than ever before. Other key contemporary words were 'union', relating either to a trade or trades union or to a political union, like Thomas Attwood's Birmingham Political Union (BPU), and 'movement', which could encompass membership of a variety of organisations, some of them differing in their specific objectives.

Within the labour movement, not yet so called, there were different entry points into Chartism. Nor once within it did old allegiances need to be cast aside. It was possible, for example, for an active working man to be both an Owenite cooperator, a trade unionist and a Chartist. Owenism, spurning political solutions, and Chartism could be alternatives, but they could also be twin activities. Many Chartist meetings were held in Owenite premises in London, Manchester and other 'localities'. 'Hall of Science', social science, was one of the Owenite addresses.

Share in 'struggle' did not always make for brotherhood. In the years leading up to the Charter, as in its last years, there were rivalries and jealousies, as there are in all politics. Dispute was more disturbing to the rank and file, however, when 'solidarity' (or 'brotherhood') was being held up as more than an ideal. Sometimes there were differences in philosophy, for instance between Owen and Paine. Thomas Attwood's views on currency questions, to which he attached prime importance – it was they that drew him into political agitation – were diametrically opposed to those of Cobbett. Place (in private) thought both of them 'absurd', one of his favourite adjectives.

Before the Charter was drafted it was in the pages of *The Northern Star* that Lovett (in a letter) described O'Connor in March 1838 as 'the great I am of politics', with O'Connor in reply impugning the motives and actions of the radical MPs who had been prepared to work on the Charter: 'I do more real work in a week than they do in a year.' One of the MPs, John Arthur Roebuck, who may have written the preamble to the Charter, was to call O'Connor a malignant and cowardly demagogue. Lovett himself was to refuse an invitation to rejoin O'Connor as secretary of the National Charter Association in 1843 on the grounds that he regarded him as 'the chief marplot in our movement in favour of the Charter; a man who by his personal conduct . . . has been the blight of democracy [a word Lovett did use] from the first moment he opened his lips as its professed advocate'.

The differences between O'Connor and O'Connell – the latter at first an ally of Attwood – went deepest, preceding all O'Connor's differences with fellow Chartists. Unlike Lovett, O'Connell was a critic of trade unions, and so long as he figured as a sympathiser with the Charter this seemed to O'Connor a liability rather than an asset. (He had other critics, however, and was, in fact, dropped by its sponsors.) None the less, when O'Connor was in gaol he supported a radical motion in Parliament to grant him and his Chartist colleagues better prison conditions.

The position of Place, never in the public eye like O'Connell, was controversial too. Lovett, unlike O'Connor, was prepared to work with and through him. In flat contradiction to O'Connor and his allies in the north, Place supported the New Poor Law Amendment Act of 1834, which cut the link between the parish and the poor and divided the country into unions each with its workhouse. For the atheist Place, as for the so-called 'philosophical radicals' who had converted him to 'Malthusianism' and who had worked hard to get the 1834 Act passed, over-population was the cause of poverty. The poor were poor because there were too many of them.

Such a 'philosophy' was anathema to Cobbett, who published his forthright views on it in *Legacy to Labourers* just before his death. It was anathema too to Oastler, who never called himself a Chartist, and initially at least thought of the publication of the Charter as part of a cunning 'Malthusian' conspiracy to substitute a political movement based on the

Charter for the social movement against the New
Poor Law. 'It is because the multitude of the people
is believed to be too great,' he argued, that Whigs –
and radicals – were enforcing 'measures hostile to
nature.'

There was, indeed, a philosophical rather than a
popular radical tinge to the Charter considered as a
document. Its form reflected the nature and
circumstances of its birth which took place in
London, not in the north of England. It was the
draft of an Act of Parliament, a bill, divided into
thirteen sections, to be presented to the House of
Commons. The first section consisted of a preamble:
the thirteenth dealt with 'penalties', with what,
would happen, for example, if electoral corruption
were to be proven or if some people had voted
twice. There was substantial practical detail on
matters like the election of paid returning officers
and the defraying of election expenses out of district
rates – a point that has recently acquired new
significance in an age of party government.
Canvassing was to be illegal, and there were to be no
public meetings on election day.

These sections of the Charter reveal a fascination with the mechanics of elections but had little to do with the sectional struggles in the country, the 'materials of convulsion', with which O'Connor had become more familiar than any other future Chartist: they recall rather the debates about the constitution in France in 1789. The word 'ought' stands out in the Preamble:

> Whereas the Commons House of Parliament now exercises in the name and on the supposed behalf of the people the power of making the laws, it *ought* [my italics], in order to fulfil with wisdom and with honesty the great duties imposed on it, to be made the faithful and accurate representative of the people's wishes, feelings and interests.

More than mechanics was involved at this point. There was a Parliamentary ideal. Attwood, who disliked intensely the existing House of Commons to which he had been elected in 1832, argued against the radical Joseph Hume's proposal to transfer it to a different place after the great fire of 1836: 'the Houses of Parliament had stood on this present site for nearly six hundred years. I hope they will stand on it for six hundred years to come.'

The Preamble of the Charter was followed by the Six Points, with universal suffrage and equal electoral districts being put first and second, and the ballot, annual parliaments and payment of Members of Parliament following later. All 'Six Cardinal Points of Radical Reform' were concerned with the House of Commons: all had a radical pedigree stretching back into the eighteenth century and sometimes even earlier. (Leave to bring in a bill in the House of Commons to establish annual Parliaments had been defeated in 1744 by only a small majority.)

There were radical MPs in 1837 who supported all or most of the Six Points – and continued to do so – but the Charter was not the product of Parliamentary radicalism, although it might have been so. The LWMA, founded by Lovett and Hetherington in June 1836, used the words 'bond of unity' in its first declaration, setting out the need to unite 'the intelligent and influential portion of the working classes in town and country' and 'to seek by every legal means to place all classes of society in possession of equal political and social rights'. The Association wanted to remain small and at its maximum consisted of only a hundred ordinary members, all working-class. Lovett was its secretary and Hetherington its treasurer. The Association also appointed thirty-five honorary members. Owen, Place, Oastler and O'Brien were among them, as were several radical MPs – and O'Connor, who had been disqualified from Parliament in 1837 for not having the requisite property qualification.

Like the Fabians later in the century the LWMA believed in research and in January 1837 it accepted an invitation from Place to hold a study group on Sunday mornings. Education was placed at the top of its objectives, as it was to be in the twentieth-century WEA: knowledge was the key to freedom. Ignorance went with poverty: it perpetuated power-lessness. Independence was compatible with poverty but not with pauperism. Statistics could be put to good use to inform and to redress. One of the first pamphlets of the Association was called *The Rotten House of Commons*; among other information (and an Address by Lovett) it provided details of the exact numbers of voters and of male inhabitants in every Parliamentary constituency. The electorate remained small after the passing of the Reform Act of 1832 – less than 850,000 from an adult male population of just over 6 million – and constituencies remained of unequal size.

This pamphlet and the brochure issued to members of the LWMA in June 1836 explained clearly why a Charter was deemed necessary:

> When we contend for an equality of political rights, it is . . . to be able to probe our social evils to their source and to apply effective remedies to prevent, instead of unjust laws to punish. We shall meet with obstacles, disappointments, and maybe with persecution, in our pursuit; but with our united exertions and perseverance we shall succeed.

Small though it was – or rather because it was kept deliberately small – the LWMA recognised the need for publicity as well as for research and its message was proclaimed and advertised around the country by 'missionaries', who included Cleave and a brilliant young orator, Henry Vincent. He was still in his twenties and was hailed as 'the Demosthenes of

Chartism', soon attracting a personal following both in England and Wales. The spoken word counted for as much as the written word in a society where there was considerable illiteracy, a point appreciated even more by O'Connor than by Lovett: O'Connor was already putting his trust not in small numbers or in behind-the-scenes meetings, favoured by Place, but in mass demonstrations. For O'Connor the platform took priority over the classroom and wherever he went, including Nottingham, which he was later to represent in Parliament, he called himself a 'Huntite', assuming the place of Hunt as a star performer.

In taking pride in calling himself a demagogue in the face of criticism, O'Connor challenged all that mattered to Lovett. The word, he told his readers later in *The Northern Star*, 'is derived from the Greek words "*demos, populos*" the people, and "*ago, duco*" to lead and means a leader of the people'. Aristocratic in bearing, not proletarian, O'Connor proclaimed himself the unpaid and ever-faithful champion of the people before the word Chartist had been coined. Members of Parliament, the Charter said, should be paid: he was not. They should be balloted for, it also said: he was self-proclaimed. 'I have a right to speak to you in the language of dictation', he told a northern crowd early in 1838, 'because of all the men (since the passing of the Reform Bill) who have represented you, both in, and out of Parliament, I alone have stood by my pledges, and supported you in your cause.'

O'Connor was as zealous in demanding 'unified organisation' as the LWMA was: 'We are not organised: we have the force, the power, but we want the organisation.' And this could be fostered, he believed, through *The Northern Star* more than through carefully researched publications. 'The power of the Press is acknowledged upon all hands', he wrote, 'and rather than oppose it, I have preferred to arm myself with it.' The arrival of the *Star* was a great weekly event. Covering not only O'Connor's activities but those of Chartists in many different places, it kept O'Connor in touch with everything that was going on. There was a two-way traffic. In an interesting note in 1839 he observed (not entirely accurately) that the airing of local grievances had hitherto been a matter of 'mere oral tradition'. Now the views and reputations of platform orators could become known far beyond 'the immediate precincts of their own locality'. Even their likenesses could be circulated.

As far as the nationalisation of protest was concerned – and O'Connor through speaking tours soon incorporated Scotland in his scene – three meetings still stand out as they did at the time. Even before *The Northern Star* was launched a huge meeting in May 1837 on Hartshead Moor in the West Riding of Yorkshire was well reported in the London press (including *The Times*) as well as in local newspapers. The factory reformer John Fielden was on the platform. So too were Stephens, Hetherington – and Owen. Yet it was O'Connor who drove home a single message. 'I am determined', he had told his huge audience, 'wherever I meet you . . . to bring forward the question of Universal Suffrage.' One published report adds – 'burst of applause, and cries of "That's it".'

Such notes of audience reaction, which often

include 'laughter', can be as revealing as digests of the speeches. Not everyone on the platform on the moor would have felt 'That's it', although at another great meeting on Hunslet Moor near Leeds in June 1838 after the Charter had been published universal suffrage was the only issue. It was there that O'Connor announced the creation of a loosely organised Northern Political Union, a very different kind of organisation from both the BPU and the LWMA.

For posterity the best-known of all meetings that proved to be 'historic' had been held at the Crown and Anchor Tavern in the Strand in London on 28 February 1837: it was chaired by Robert Hartwell, a London radical who figured prominently not only in the history of Chartism but also in earlier and later labour history. According to O'Brien, who wrote an enthusiastic account of it, 'four thousand democrats at least', among them O'Connor, had been present. (Never trust press estimates of numbers.) 'Lift up your democratic heads, my friends', O'Brien began his account. 'Look proud and be merry. I was at a meeting on Tuesday night which does one's heart

good to think on.' Five of the Six Points subsequently incorporated in the Charter figured in a
petition presented there: the only missing one was
payment of Members of Parliament, and for annual
Parliaments the phrase was substituted 'short
Parliaments of fixed duration, not to exceed three
years'.

Other meetings called by the LWMA followed in
London in late May and June 1837 between
representatives of the LWMA and radical MPs,
among them Joseph Hume, thirteen years older
than Lovett, first elected to Westminster in 1812,
and Perronet Thompson, author of a celebrated
Catechism of the Corn Laws (1826) which went
through twenty editions. That was the point when
the LWMA would have left much to the
Parliamentary radicals had it had the ability to
determine the timing. A committee of six MPs and
six representatives of the LWMA was formed to draw
up the draft of a bill to secure the listed points.
Before it could get to work, however, the death of
King William IV entailed a general election in July
1837; many radicals lost their seats, and the

committee was stopped from completing the bill. The result, therefore, was that the bill, now called the Charter, was drafted not by a joint committee, which included MPs, but by Lovett and substantially (according to his own account) by Place, who was probably responsible for the excessive detail to be found in it but who appreciated the importance of timing as much as any northern Chartist.

What brought different provincial groups to support the Charter, including those militants in the north who were at first suspicious of it, was the stimulus of economic distress, and Place was aware of this while disapproving of what many local leaders considered to be its main cause. It has been a commonplace for historians to argue that what lay behind the Charter – social distress, social discontent and the demand for social trans- formation – was the key to its immediate appeal. The concern everywhere was for what the Charter would *do* or rather enable Chartists to do if they gained the Six Points. They might disagree on the answers they gave – for example, when they turned to the Corn Laws (some were repealers, others protectionists) – but they were united in putting the Charter first. It became a unifying document.

How the British national struggle to secure it began – and how it was waged through different phases – are the themes of the next chapter. Initially, however, the Six Points themselves were expounded differently by northern factory reformers and rebels against the New Poor Law who sought to 'make the Charter our own', and by those members of the LWMA, artisans rather than handloom weavers or factory operatives, who were determined 'to make the principles of democracy as respectable in practice as they are just in theory'.

The fiery Lancashire opponent of the New Poor Law, the independent Methodist minister Stephens, was to define the aims of the Charter memorably in purely social terms: universal suffrage was the means to secure the right of 'every working man in the land' to have:

> a good coat to his back, a comfortable abode in which to shelter himself and his family, a good dinner upon his table, and no more work than is necessary for keeping him in good health and as much wages for that work as would keep him

in plenty and afford him all the blessings of life which a reasonable man could desire.

Stephens differed from the LWMA leaders almost as much on ends as on means. It was the difference on means, however, which mattered most – in his case and in that of others.

In January 1838, before the Charter was drafted, he had told an audience at Newcastle, another great centre of mass demonstrations and birthplace of another Chartist newspaper, *The Northern Liberator*, that:

> if the people who produce all wealth could not be allowed, according to God's word, to have the kindly fruits of the earth which . . . they had raised by the sweat of their brow, then war to the knife with their enemies, who were the enemies of God.

Later in 1838, after the Charter had been published, Stephens repeated to a Wigan audience in his home territory of Lancashire:

> The firelock must come first and the vote afterwards. Universal [suffrage] might be a very fine thing, but as yet it was all in the moon.

Stephens was addressing an audience many of whom knew that pikes were on sale and where to get them.

This was never O'Connor's language, although from the start he was prepared to proclaim 'the right of every man' to bear arms in the defence of justice and was to go on to threaten the government with physical force if all else failed. He explained to his *Northern Star* readers before and after the Charter was published that only 'laws made by all would be respected by all' and claimed (however unconvincingly for posterity) that universal suffrage would:

> at once change the whole character of society from a state of watchfulness, doubt and suspicion, to that of brotherly love, reciprocal interest and universal contentment . . . Give us, then, the only remedy for all our social and political maladies; make every man his own doctor by placing the restorative in hand, which is universal suffrage!!!

Whatever the language being heard from the platform, O'Connor, responding to the mood of his audience, cast a spell over them. In an age of localism, not least in London itself where he chose to draw on metropolitan radical tradition, there were difficulties in communicating between different associations in localities as different as Greenwich and Southwark; and in Lancashire there were marked differences between, for example, Preston and Bury. There were similar differences inside Yorkshire, which along with Lancashire, Durham and Northumberland figured on the national mental map as 'the North', an area in total contrast to the south. Birmingham belonged to neither. Nor, of course, did Glasgow and Edinburgh, which pursued their own civic rivalry as they still do. The map of South Wales was still in the course of being filled in. It was the genius of O'Connor not only to establish interconnections but also to achieve an unprecedented degree of political coordination once the Charter had been published; and although he had nothing at all to do with its drafting, it was he more than anyone else who ensured that it would be adopted as a set of demands that soon acquired as much symbolic as practical significance.

O'Connor was not alone in seeing the need for communication and coordination: it was recognised both by the LWMA and by the BPU, which, like the LWMA, sent out 'missionaries'. But it was he who cleverly, if often dubiously, overshadowed and supplanted local leaders in their own localities, men who were often tied to their own 'causes', like Thomas Attwood in Birmingham (currency reform), or Stephens in Lancashire (the end of the New Poor Law), or Ebenezer Elliott in Sheffield (Corn Law repeal), or the Revd Patrick Brewster in Edinburgh (a moral crusader, whose pulpit was his platform). In the struggle that followed the publication of the Charter many old organisations were to disappear, including the LWMA, which died when Chartism was born. The anti-Poor Law movement and the BPU were soon to die also.

Before that, however, a second Chartist document emerged from Birmingham and was to become as well known in its time as the Charter. It was a document dealing with principles and not with details, a short National Petition, drafted by one man, R.K. Douglas, editor of the *Birmingham Journal*. Douglas was a friend of Attwood: familiar with the long history of formal petitions to Parliament, he took great pains with the writing of his and introduced it in person to a huge Birmingham audience on 16 August 1838. Already on 21 May a great meeting had been held in Glasgow at which both Charter and Petition were made public, and the planning of a National Convention, itself not a new idea, had begun: it was to be attended by delegates from different localities.

The Petition, which focused on distress but left out Attwood's currency remedy, was something more than a sonorous accompaniment to the Charter. It was an invitation to working men everywhere (and at first to others) to join in a great endeavour (Douglas had an eye to posterity as well as to his contemporaries). Lovett proudly printed the Petition years later as an appendix to his *Life and Struggles*:

> We are bowed down under a load of taxes . . . our trades are trembling on the verge of bankruptcy; our workmen are starving; capital brings no profit, and labour no remuneration; the home of the artificer is desolate, and the warehouse of the pawnbroker is full; the workhouse is crowded, and the manufactory is deserted.
>
> We have looked on every side, we have searched diligently in order to find out the causes of a distress so sore and so long continued. We can discover none in Nature or in

> Providence. Heaven has dealt graciously with the people; but the foolishness of our rulers has made the goodness of God of none effect.

This was Birmingham language, highly acceptable in Scotland, but treated with some impatience in the north of England where huge torchlight meetings were being held to proclaim the Charter and to elect delegates to the Convention. As one Newcastle-upon-Tyne Chartist, James Ayr, put it at a meeting called in June 1838 – and Birmingham had family connections with Newcastle through Attwood's brother – this was to be the last document in the shape of a petition that would ever be presented. Ayr was not alone in stressing the word 'last'. Nor was he alone in forecasting trouble ahead. In a private letter – and not in a speech on a public platform – Vincent, the brilliant young Chartist orator, told *his* brother that 'if we fail in our present efforts to obtain a peaceful Radical change, one of the most bloody revolutions the world has ever seen will occur'.

THREE

Narrative

With hindsight we know that that revolution never came and that in 1848, a year of European revolutions, Britain and Russia were two countries that never had one. It is necessary, however, in dealing with the varied fortunes of Chartism in the decade after 1838 to concentrate not on what would happen but on what was happening – more dramatic (often with a touch of theatre about it) than contemporary events in any other European country.

Just when to begin the narrative is not easy to decide. Even the briefest of accounts should not start with 4 February 1839, the calling of the National Convention, any more than it should end on 10 April 1848. As has been shown, the Chartist story began long before the Charter. Where to begin is no more straightforward. Birmingham provides a quite different entry point from London, Manchester or Newcastle. In Manchester, a city distinct from Birmingham in economic and social structure, most memories lingered on the 'massacre of Peterloo' when the Tories had put down 'the people' in 1819. The passing of Six Acts (1819) curtailing civil freedom preceded the Chartists' Six Points by nearly twenty years.

One tempting starting point in both place and time is Birmingham, 1775, the year of the Boulton and Watt patent for Watt's steam engine, for there would have been no Chartism without industrialisation and the emergence of the 'industrious classes' as they were first called. Yet even before Boulton and Watt the first textile mills were already operating, driven by water power, and even before that steam power was being used to pump water out of coal mines near Newcastle. Ironically, steam power was being used less in Birmingham in 1838 than in most industrial cities: it was a place of small workshops and small employers, not of large factories and rich 'capitalists'.

If the emphasis is placed not on economic but on political history, the time-scale changes and thanks to E.P. Thompson's seminal study *The Making of the English Working Class* (1963) we can trace not only the emergence of a sense of class but the persistence of an unbroken radical tradition. There were many Chartists who looked back to Tom Paine and Major John Cartwright, the Nottinghamshire radical, and many of them had taken part in eighteenth- and nineteenth-century radical activity. Cartwright's pamphlet *Take Your Choice* was published in 1776, the year of American Independence and of Adam Smith's *Wealth of Nations*, one year after the Boulton and Watt patent: it argued that 'making our Parliaments *annual* and our representation *equal* can neither of them, in any sense . . . be styled innovations. *Both of them were the antient practice of the constitution.*'

The French Revolution opened up new vistas and fascinated Chartists like O'Brien and Harney, the latter assertively proud of his republicanism and his internationalism. Yet an indigenous 'patriot' strand was strong in Chartism, and one of the delegates to the Chartist Convention moved a resolution that 'the present movement, being essentially English, and not having in view any theoretical innovations, but a recurrence to the first principles of the Saxon Constitution', deprecated any language or expression that 'would appear to associate our objects to those of the French Revolution'. Even Harney resorted to a distinctively English framework of reference when seeking election to the same Convention at Derby as an avowed 'physical force Chartist':

> Time was when every Englishman had a musket in his cottage, and along with it hung a flitch of bacon. Now there is no flitch of bacon for there is no musket; let the musket be restored and the flitch of bacon will soon follow.

However far back the historian goes in choosing his framework of analysis, the most obvious opening date for the Chartist story in its political context is the Reform Act of 1832 that enlarged the electorate and redistributed constituencies; and the right place to begin, once again, is Birmingham, the provincial city which claimed (never convincingly for subsequent historians) that the pressure of its

Political Union enabled, at times forced, the Whigs to press on with their Reform Bill, 'the whole Bill and nothing but the Bill'.

In straight political terms it was not so much the limited nature of the Reform Act of 1832 – explained in detail in the LWMA's *The Rotten House of Commons* – that stirred working-class politics in 1837 and 1838 as the memories of the two-year struggle to get the Act passed. The first real political drama came then, with the 'middle classes' seeming to set the pace. It was a struggle which also revealed many of the differences within the working classes which were subsequently expressed in Chartism. Orator Hunt opposed the Bill. Oastler, Tory then as much as radical, thought it a 'Grey trick . . . nothing but a delusion'.

Historians have often used a different word, 'disillusionment', never quite the right one to employ, to describe the mood *after* 1832, and they have traced the sequence of Whig legislation from an Irish Coercion Bill, their first measure, attacked by the BPU and by O'Connell, through the Poor Law Amendment Act of 1834 (approved of by O'Connell) and on

through the reduction of the stamp duty in 1836 from
4*d* to 1*d*. This too was supported by O'Connell: after
making a political compact with the Whigs, which
meant that they granted him concessions, he was
unwilling in return to criticise them.

The mounting popular anger as this legislative
sequence continued, anger not shared everywhere,
was restrained by economic conditions. A sequence
of good harvests and an upturn in trade and
industry, promoted what was called, never entirely
accurately, 'prosperity'. It was known to be difficult
'to agitate a man on a full stomach', a Cobbett
phrase that was picked up by Attwood; and
although, like the Reform Act itself, the prosperity
was limited in its scope and uneven from occupation
to occupation (handloom weavers continued their
economic and social descent) and from place to
place (Nottingham was less prosperous than Derby),
it was real enough to promote trade union action.
The price of wheat fell from 63*s* a quarter when the
Reform Bill was passed to only 36*s* at the end of
1835. Trade union action, however, was strictly
limited by the law and ultimately prevented by it.

It was during these years that Owen's dream of a Grand National Consolidated Trades Union (GNCTU) took shape, with some of the language relating to it anticipating the language of the Chartist Convention. 'There are two Parliaments in London', the *Crisis* observed in 1834, 'and we have no hesitation in saying that the Trades Parliament is by far the most important, and will in the course of a year or two be the more influential.' This was as wild a prediction as any made during the Chartist agitation. The GNCTU collapsed, and when six Dorchester labourers, now remembered as 'the Tolpuddle martyrs', were transported as criminals to Australia for organising a trade union in 1833, several months before the GNCTU failed, this in itself generated new political action. For many disgruntled workers the enemy was less the employers than the Whig government.

It was the government, not business, that was blamed again both for the dramatic change in economic circumstances following the end of the run of good harvests and a financial crisis with international origins in 1836, sometimes described at the time as 'a great panic'. A consequent deepening depression in 1837 affecting workers and employers alike – in Douglas's words to be 'sore and long continued' – was to reach its trough in 1842, the second landmark year in the history of Chartism.

In 1838 the revived BPU, which had been founded in a year of 'distress', 1829, – *before* the Whigs returned to power in 1830 – reflected middle-class disillusionment (in this case the right word) with the record of Whig government before turning on 7 November 1837 to universal suffrage as a necessary requirement for a change in official policy. The monetary economic theory, which its leaders believed explained fluctuations, looked back to 1819, in this case not to Peterloo but to Peel's Act to restore the gold currency that had been suspended during the wars against revolutionary France and Napoleon. For Attwood that was where Britain's troubles had really started. The Act guaranteed fluctuations in output and income, with recurring cyclical 'distress'.

In changing circumstances in 1838 LWMA overtures, once looked upon with suspicion by the

BPU, were now warmly welcomed in Birmingham but there was a feeling of pride that Birmingham, not London, was once more taking the political initiative. With pride went political elation as 'the glorious flag of the Union flew once more in the middle of the city and meetings were held at the *Old Place* [Newhall Hill] under our old Leader [Attwood] for the old Cause'. There was a good old cry too – 'Peace, Law, Order, Loyalty, Union' – a very different cry from that of Stephens in Lancashire.

Attwood was just as convinced as O'Connor was that the success of 'the old Cause' depended on winning support outside as well as inside Birmingham. Numbers mattered far more to him than to Lovett, and he liked great gatherings. It was with his blessing that the BPU, like the LWMA, was soon sending out missionaries urging the creation of what he called 'unions of the people' and what O'Connor called 'a great chain'. At first Attwood seemed to be in a strong position, as O'Connor recognised. Even Place, who disliked him, acknowledged this.

The first link in the great chain was forged between Birmingham and Glasgow, metropolis of mercantile and industrial Clydeside, by John Collins, a working man and BPU missionary, although Glasgow had already been visited by O'Connor on one of his political pilgrimages. The climax came on 21 May 1838 when a huge meeting, addressed by Attwood and by LWMA representatives, was held on Glasgow Green. Both Charter and Petition were now ready and there was discipline as well as excitement when no fewer than seventy trade unions, bearing their banners, arrived at the meeting in ordered processions. As in most other centres of discontent, there had been a local issue in Glasgow with national implications: wage cuts in the winter of 1836/7 had triggered off bitter strikes against a background not of relative prosperity but of intense distress. The trial in January 1838 of eighteen leaders of the Operative Spinners' Union and their sentence to transportation provoked as sharp a political reaction as had the trial and transportation of the Dorchester labourers.

Some of the language used in defence of the trade unionists was as violent as the language used in the north of England against the 'Satanic' New

Poor Law of 1834. Thus, Augustus Harding Beaumont, editor first of *The Radical* and then of Newcastle's *Northern Liberator*, talked at another Glasgow meeting of war to the death with 'the aristocracy, that we might show how ready we are to shed our blood'.

Beaumont, who died later in 1838, was a genuine revolutionary, looking back, like Harney, to the French Revolution, as did the Scot Dr John Taylor, who at the same meeting said that it was 'high time to lay down the spade and take up the sword'. On the other side there was the fear of revolution: Sir Archibald Alison, Sheriff of Lanarkshire, who had ordered the arrest of the Glasgow trade unionists, was a high Tory, who wrote a widely read anti-revolutionary *History of Europe*.

For the most part it was Whig misrule, not Tory prejudice, that was in the spotlight in 1837 and in 1838, and once again it was Whig actions – and inactions – that generated anger out of discontent. While the Charter and the Petition were in course of preparation, Melbourne, the Whig Prime Minister, decisively turned down Attwood's currency scheme on 2 November; and at the opening of the new Parliament, when the Queen's speech offered no answers to economic and social distress, Lord John Russell, Whig Home Secretary, made an anti-radical speech that even Melbourne thought was unwise. He declared bluntly that he would never be a party to the ballot and that he would never reform the Reform Act. 'Finality Jack', as he now came to be called (he was to prove in the long run that he was not), obviously cared no more in 1837 about the sensibilities of radical MPs at Westminster than about popular protest outside Parliament. In the country there was fury. Attwood was not alone in judging that if the Queen's speech had been made by the Emperor of China 'it could not have had less reference to the wants of the British nation'.

The inadequacies – or abominations – of the Westminster Parliament were in the forefront as the different Chartist 'localities' set about choosing their representatives to their own 'Convention of the Industrious Classes' (no more a new idea than the Six Points) that was to assemble in parallel to the Westminster Parliament on 4 February 1839. There was a thrill in choosing delegates, the first opportunity for doing so; perhaps there was less of a thrill in paying 'rent' (an idea borrowed from O'Connell) to meet members' costs. But beyond the excitement there were high expectations, far too high, of what the People's Parliament would achieve. There were also ominous divisions inside the Convention, particularly on the question, which most members wanted to postpone, of what they would do when (a better word than if) the Petition was turned down.

Some of the elected delegates thought of themselves as members of a 'real Parliament', even of an alternative government – and a superior one – to that in Whitehall: several put 'M.C.' after their names. They had been chosen quite differently from MPs, however, even if there were as many anomalies in their modes of election as there were in the national system. There was no balloting; Chartist 'constituencies' were unequal; London and Birmingham were over-represented; some delegates were paid, others not; sixteen of them attended as representatives of more than one constituency,

O'Brien for no fewer than five – London, Leigh (Lancashire), Stockport, Newport and the Isle of Wight. Dorset returned George Lovelace, one of the Tolpuddle martyrs, but he could only afford to attend for less than a week. Among the members who did attend were some who thought of themselves, as Russell judged them, not as a Parliament but as a representative body lobbying for signatures to the Petition and making arrangements for its presentation to the other Parliament.

At first most members of the Convention wished to paper over this division of approach, and J.P. Cobbett, lawyer son of a great father, withdrew from the Convention at once after he won little support for his resolutions asserting that the *sole* purpose of the convention was to superintend the presentation of the Petition. The Chairman on the first morning was R.K. Douglas, the Petition's drafter, but he also subsequently took no part in its proceedings. Nor did his other Birmingham colleagues, who knew a great deal about organisation and had collected more 'rent' than any other 'constituency'.

Douglas particularly resented that too little effort had been made to secure signatures. He had contemplated as many as 6 million: in fact, there were only just over half a million. Yet there was another reason why he and the Birmingham delegates (except Collins) withdrew on 28 March. They objected to the language of physical force used at a side meeting held at the Crown and Anchor Tavern on 16 March 1839 (and, indeed, in the Convention itself).

The withdrawal of the BPU leaders cannot be explained simply on the grounds that they were 'middle class' and most of the members of the Convention were 'working class'. In fact, a majority of the first fifty-three delegates (twenty-nine) were described by Place, if somewhat unsatisfactorily, as 'middle class': they were not paid wages. Their replacements, however, were usually more obviously 'working class'. The Anglican vicar, the Revd Arthur Wade, for example, was replaced by James Woodhouse, a framework knitter. The West Riding had been more prepared for members' imprisonment than for their withdrawal: they chose three substitute delegates before the Convention opened.

As the devoted and scrupulously loyal secretary of the Convention, elected on its opening day, Lovett bore great responsibilities, but, like many later secretaries in the labour movement, he discharged them as a secretary not as a leader. If there was a leader it was O'Connor, and while there was no O'Connorite group in the Convention – nor was there ever anything that could be called 'O'Connorism' (Lovett's word) – the presence of 'the Lion of Freedom' was always felt. He tried to keep likely troublemakers in order, sometimes by flattering them, and reserved his criticism for 'intruders and meddlers'. More important, he attempted to ensure that members of the Convention kept in touch with their 'constituencies', a priority when the date of the presentation of the National Petition, first set for 5 May, was delayed. The country would look upon the Charter as a 'mere fiction', he told the members of the Convention in that month, unless they gave a lead.

By then, however, they were in no position to do so. Half of them had either withdrawn or were not attending Convention sessions. One delegate from the north, Joseph Wood from Bolton, might well have been declared guilty of treason: he had become a Poor Law Guardian. Another, the once militant gentleman doctor W.S. Villiers Sankey from Edinburgh who withdrew in May, now warned that 'the people of Scotland were too calm, too prudent and too humane to peril [their] cause on bloodshed'. Meanwhile, missionaries sent out to different parts of the country where Chartism was not strong were reporting that they were receiving a hostile reception. By then too there was far more disagreement than agreement on the Convention floor, only temporarily cast aside on 7 May when the National Petition, now 3 miles long, was escorted on a decorated cart to Fielden's home. It was a real fiasco when Fielden was found not to be there and the Petition had to be carried to Attwood's house instead.

Attwood, now called upon to be Chartism's Parliamentary champion, cannot have been happy about this outcome, but he agreed to present the National Petition while refusing to introduce a bill based on it (200 of the 600 proposed seats in the reformed House of Commons would have been in

Ireland). As it was, for reasons beyond their control, he and Fielden could not present the Petition to Parliament until 12 July, a month after the Convention had decided to move from London to Birmingham, a decision that would have pleased Attwood had Birmingham remained under the influence of the BPU. The Convention's resolution to move there, a close one rescinding a previous decision, was prompted mainly by government action: on Melbourne's advice Parliament was dissolved on 11 May 1839 (after a close Parliamentary vote which led the Prime Minister to resign) and it was now clear that the National Petition could not be presented. Melbourne was soon back, but the Chartist chronology had completely changed.

Thirty-five members of the Convention travelled by rail to Birmingham, and once there issued a manifesto setting out a wide range of 'ulterior measures', on which members had hitherto been divided for an almost equally wide range of reasons. They included a 'sacred month' (or general strike), not a new idea (Attwood had thought of it; so, too, had a better informed working-class pamphleteer,

William Benbow); the conversion of paper money into gold; the withdrawal of funds from savings banks; abstinence from the purchase of excised goods; and exclusive dealings only with sympathetic shopkeepers. There was much talk too of the nomination of Chartist candidates on the hustings at the next general election and of arming, a particularly threatening proposal to the authorities in a city where armaments were made.

Having uttered at last, the Convention then adjourned until 1 July, leaving the constituencies free to act as they wished, subject, perhaps, to the advice of *The Northern Star* – 'Let no arms of any description be paraded. Let your words be carefully chosen.' Rallies, sometimes 'simultaneous', now took place in different parts of the country. Coinciding as they did with Whitsuntide, a favourite time for mass gatherings of all kinds in the north of England, they were inevitably excitable and in places desperate, but there was no violent confrontation. Not surprisingly, there were torchlight meetings where, as at Ashton, firearms were periodically let off.

In the absence of an adequate national or provincial

police system, the government had already taken several important decisions in the name of law and order. It had recalled troops from Ireland to serve in the north of England, and in February 1839 the Army had appointed Sir Charles Napier to take command of the Northern District from headquarters in Nottingham, with over 5,000 scattered troops at his disposal. In May 1839 by royal proclamation the government forbade drilling, authorised the Lord Lieutenants of the counties to arm special constables, and allowed magistrates to arrest armed Chartists. In August Russell was to issue more specific instructions to them.

The appointment of Napier, a loyal and distinguished soldier who was to be transferred to India after two years in the north and who was to be a pallbearer at Wellington's funeral, was particularly interesting and revealing. He was sympathetic to the Chartists, and, like Oastler, he believed that 'manufactures produced corrupt[ed] morals, bad health, uncertain wages and dependence on the foreign market'. In politics he was a radical, sympathetic to the Chartists and objecting equally to

'Whig imbecility' and to 'Tory injustice': 'The doctrine of slowly reforming when men are starving is of all things the most silly; famishing men cannot wait.' None the less, Napier made it clear to Chartists that he would use force if they themselves did, force which, disciplined as it was, would be bound to prevail. He saw no real revolutionary thread, except in Manchester, to which he moved his Command headquarters in the summer of 1839. 'I would never allow them to charge me with their pikes or even march ten miles', he told his superiors, 'without mauling them with cannon and charging them with cavalry.'

As for the local magistrates, whom Napier believed were 'in a fuss', many of them had not known what to make of Chartist 'disturbances', real or feared, in 1838 and early 1839. In particular, they had been as uncertain as many Chartists themselves were about what 'line' to take towards the relationship between violent words and violence in action. Thus, for example, the Mayor of Penzance, appealing to Russell in March 1839, asked 'your Lordship' for instructions that would enable him to respond to pressure from the 'upper classes of society' to effect the 'desirable object' of suppressing Chartist meetings in future.

Russell (with Peterloo in mind) had been unwilling to approve magisterial action if violence were restricted to talk, and he was not present in cabinet when the decision was taken to arrest Stephens in December 1838. He was already using an elaborate spy system (as his predecessors had done), and in February 1839 authorised the opening of the correspondence of Vincent, Hartwell, Richardson and Wade (but not that of O'Connor or Lovett). He could easily dispose of Attwood in verbal contest on the floor of the Commons, but he could not prevent street violence in Birmingham.

The Convention had returned to Birmingham on 1 July following its early summer break and was in session on 4 July when it was reported that a posse of London policemen, called in by the Mayor and the Birmingham magistrates, who had given due warning, had tried in vain to disperse a Bull Ring crowd. Troops had been summoned, and two members of the Convention, Peter M'Douall and John Taylor, had been arrested. There were further disturbances on the 5th. To the Chartists this seemed to be the signal for a crackdown, and a placard condemning the actions of the magistrates and police as 'a wanton, flagrant and unjust outrage' was posted in the city on 6 July. It was signed by Lovett and Collins, acting Chairman of the Convention, who were themselves arrested in turn. Once more – but now with alarming urgency – the question of 'ulterior measures' was in the forefront, now a practical, not a theoretical, question given added point by a spate of arrests of Chartists across the country. The arrests overshadowed Attwood's presentation of the Petition to Parliament on 12 July when it was turned down by 235 votes to 46 – Parliamentary finality.

Vincent's arrest in May, following that of Stephens in December 1838, had prepared the way; in addition the Judge presiding over Monmouth Assizes pronounced for the first time that the Convention was an illegal body and warned that if any attempt was made to induce others to secure the Charter by force those doing so would lay themselves open to charges of high treason. To militant Chartists this meant that 'the mask of constitutional liberty' was now finally 'thrown aside'. Taken to court, those Chartists who pleaded guilty to the charges brought against them were usually bound over. There was no such treatment, however, for those who had carried firearms or for leaders who were thought to be inflaming crowds that otherwise might not have been threatening.

An arbitrary element in dealing with particular individuals was inevitable. It is surprising that neither Harney nor Taylor faced trial and imprisonment after being arrested: Napier thought the latter the most dangerous of all the Chartists. However, Napier also made it clear how foolish he considered those people who maintained that arresting and imprisoning O'Connor would destroy the movement. As it was, O'Connor did not escape arrest but it was not until mid-March 1840 that he was tried at York Assizes for seditious libel (his own writing and that of other writers in *The Northern Star*) and in May 1840, after impressively conducting his own defence, he was sentenced to eighteen months' imprisonment.

There was considerable variation in the lapse of time between arrests and sentences: Stephens, the first 'martyr', was not called up for trial until 15 August 1839 – at the same Assizes as M'Douall and more than eight months after his arrest. Lovett and Collins were tried in the same month and each was sentenced to a year's imprisonment. All in all, as an official report of 1840 was to reveal, 476 men and women who had been tried for 'Chartist offences' were being held in prison in the winter of 1840. They were not the last. Taking the years from 1839 to 1848 as a whole, more than 3,500 Chartists were tried (some of them more than once).

For the authorities, as for historians, the trials were more than instruments of repression: they opened a window on Chartism, enabling an assessment of the extent of the 'Chartist threat'. For the Chartists themselves, the trials provided an opportunity for self-justification and, if followed by prison sentences, to acquire status: on coming out of gaol amid huge popular demonstrations those who were well known could themselves demonstrate that they had graduated in agitation.

The trials were not solely responsible for the collapse of the Convention in the autumn of 1839. Never short on political and social rhetoric, it had seldom behaved like the alternative People's Parliament that some of its members had claimed it to be. One example stands out. By taking up, then abandoning, the idea of a 'sacred month' (the subject of many split votes), the Convention created confusion. To very poor unemployed Chartists a 'sacred month' would have added to their distress. Only to ideologues did it really appeal. Yet to change course, as the Convention did, was to expose itself to criticism from Chartist sympathisers and even from Chartists. Thus, the *Champion*, a Cobbettite anti-O'Connor paper that was soon to merge with *The Northern Liberator*, ended an article on 1 September in block capitals: 'THE NATIONAL PETITION WAS NOT A FAILURE: THE CONVENTION IS.'

None the less, O'Connor could boast – and it was a boast – that the Convention had 'forced a consideration of our principles upon the monarch; upon both Houses of Parliament; upon the judges of the land [this was true]; upon all the states of

Europe; upon the Press [only partially true]; and, above, all, upon the people themselves.' Even at the last stage in its story there were some Chartists who did not wish the Convention to dissolve itself, and the decision to do so on 6 September was taken only on the Chairman's casting vote. The Chairman was John Frost, until recently a magistrate (deposed by Russell) and a former Mayor of Newport. He has passed down into history not for his casting vote but for his involvement in the Newport Rising of 4 November 1839, a rare 'physical force' event even in the Chartist story, still difficult fully to explain.

There was apparent calm in Wales in late August and early September when magistrates were reporting to the Home Office that Chartism was, in decline, but behind the scenes there was drilling as there was in Lancashire and Yorkshire. It was ominous for the authorities that mass demonstrations had given way to small secret meetings. On Saturday 2 November a brief paragraph in the *Monmouthshire Merlin*, a local Welsh newspaper, was headed 'Extinction of Chartism'. (It was reporting a speech by the Attorney General.) The following night, a few thousand Welsh Chartists started a march on Newport, a march that had been planned but which ended in Chartist disaster: a lament, described as 'a mournful ditty' related what it called 'the sad disasters of the day'.

There was shooting at an inn; who started it was not – and is not – certain, and more than twenty Chartists were killed by troops. The failure of the effort and the arrest of Frost and a number of other marchers – and their subsequent sentence to death (later commuted to transportation for life) – seemed decisive proof to most Chartists that they were in no position to secure their objectives through physical force. Yet there were 'after-outbreaks', and passions were high enough to ensure that Newport was not the end of the story. For the *Dublin Review* it was important to note, even to boast, that of the people indicted in Wales only one was an Irishman.

There were indeed other places besides Newport where the idea of using physical force was seriously contemplated in the autumn of 1839 and the winter of 1839/40, and there were some Chartists, forming a kind of national network, who knew about the planning of the march on Newport before it took place. Bradford was one centre. Newcastle was another: there Thomas Ainge Devyr, who was to migrate to the United States, was awaiting a signal. Birmingham was in the middle, awaiting the signal first. How much O'Connor himself knew is uncertain: he was away in Ireland from 5 October to 2 November. In the event, whatever the strength of the network, Newport was not associated with any general insurrection. O'Connor did not believe in one. Significantly too there was no unity of purpose among the Newport marchers themselves.

The three ringleaders in the Newport Rising were charged with high treason and sentenced to death, and had they been put to death rather than transported (they owed the alteration in their treatment not to the government but to the judges) there might have been a bloody sequel. As it was, with so many Chartist leaders in gaol, sporadic outbreaks of violence, community orientated, had no chance of success. The most serious were at Dewsbury and Sheffield, and it was in Sheffield that a martyr was produced, Samuel Holberry. He died in gaol on 21 June 1840 and his funeral, recounted in ballads, was a huge public event. In most of the country, there was less talk of physical force than of Chartist reorganisation. It became the new watchword.

There were radically different ways of approaching reorganisation, some of them outside the law, and these included the most constitutional as well as the most insurrectionary proposals. All except the last were canvassed in the Chartist Press, all subject to O'Connor's scrutiny. 'Organise, organise, organise' was M'Douall's advice: 'There should have been a power behind the Convention, great enough, terrible enough, to have made it dangerous for the government to arrest the least of its members.'

The first plans emerged from Scotland: they placed an emphasis on 'moral Chartism' and argued for abandonment of the idea of Conventions, still very much alive after the failure of the 1839 Convention. (There were several mini-Conventions in 1840.) The most revolutionary plans, like that published by an anonymous 'Republican', also rejected the idea of open Conventions, envisaging a network of secret cells controlled by a 'Great Central and Secret Directory': there had already been talk before and after Newport of a 'Committee of Public Safety'. The most meticulously detailed proposals were prepared by Lovett and Collins while *they* were in gaol and published in 1840 under the title *Chartism: A New Organisation of the People*. The plan for a 'National Association of the United Kingdom for promoting the Political and Social Improvement of the People' was detailed enough to include specimens of lesson cards to be used in schools and adults' evening classes.

O'Connor dismissed all this as 'knowledge Chartism', putting his trust in the National Charter Association (NCA), brought into existence in a Manchester tavern in July 1840: Marx and Engels considered it 'the first working man's party the world ever produced'. Association members paid subscriptions and held membership cards, and dues were levied on its branches. Striking progress was made. By February 1841 there were eighty branches in the localities, by October 204, by December 282, when there were said to be 20,000 members, and by the following April 350. There was also a national executive that included M'Douall. The Treasurer was Abel Heywood, a Manchester bookseller, who ten years later was handling 10 per cent of the national trade in popular publications. He was to play a prominent part in local government, as significant numbers of Chartists did, and would be remembered as 'Father of Manchester Corporation'.

Mounting distress (and the revival of the Chartist Press) added to the mass appeal of the NCA, giving point to O'Connor's most serious objection to Lovett's plan that it 'implicitly acknowledge[d] a standard of some sort of learning, education or information as a necessary qualification to entitle a man to his political rights'. But argument continued among Chartists about O'Connor's own tactics, particularly when he supported Tories against Whigs first at a Nottingham by-election and then at the general election of 1841, won by Peel. This led to an argument with O'Brien: 'Vote for a Tory merely [to] keep out a Whig! Vote for a villain . . . to get rid of another villain. No, damn me! If I do . . .'

O'Connor totally distrusted not only Whigs but also the Anti-Corn Law League, which was to gain in strength and influence between 1841 and the repeal of the Corn Laws in 1846; the fact that O'Connell seemed to have a hand in the process was to him decisive. Meanwhile, in 1842 a new Chartist Convention was elected – this time by ballot – and signatures were collected for a new Petition, which condemned the national debt, expenditures on the royal family, long factory hours and, still on the agenda, the New Poor Law. No fewer than 3,317,752 signatures were claimed. History seemed to be repeating itself – with the usual kind of modifications, when after being introduced to the Commons on 20 April 1842 by Thomas Slingsby Duncombe, the Petition was rejected by 287 votes to 49.

The Parliamentary vote meant that once again the Chartists leaders were faced with the question of what to do next. 'Ulterior measures' were no longer listed and given degrees of priority. Instead, both the National Charter Association, dominated by O'Connor, and other Chartist groups had to deal with sympathetic, if sometimes patronising, middle-class overtures, what O'Connor's biographer James Epstein has called 'the middle-class challenge'. The first overtures in Leeds preceded the presentation of the Petition: a Parliamentary Reform Association (pledged both to extension of the suffrage and repeal of the Corn Laws) was formed there in May 1830, the month when O'Connor went to gaol. It was backed by the *Leeds Times*, then edited by Samuel Smiles, a radical who enters most of the history books in a very different guise, and was contemptuously described by O'Connor as 'the Leeds Fox and Goose Club'.

Out of gaol, O'Connor was equally contemptuous of a Birmingham body created in 1841, the Complete Suffrage Union (CSU), the most serious attempt to bring together middle-class and working-class supporters of political and economic reform. Not surprisingly, Birmingham, where there was a tradition, recently challenged, of class union, was the place of origin, but the leader in the initiative was not an Attwoodite but a Quaker, Joseph Sturge, a corn factor, who had the backing of Edward Miall, radical editor of the weekly *Nonconformist*, and two of the key figures in the Anti-Corn Law League, John

Bright and its future historian Archibald Prentice. A pro-Sturge declaration was carried at an Edinburgh meeting of the League in January 1842 and at a London meeting at the Crown and Anchor Tavern on 11 February 1842 at which Hetherington and Lovett were present. 'If Mr Sturge and his friends would inquire into the Charter as a whole', Lovett promised, 'he should be prepared to give up points that were proved to be non-essential, and by these means there would be a chance of a cordial union between the middle and working classes.'

If Cobden was unhappy about the prospect, considering that Corn Law repeal was the One Point for which to strive, O'Connor was dismissive: he called supporters of the new Union 'Complete Suffrage Humbugs'. Yet embryonic branches of the Union were formed in different parts of Britain in places as far apart as Aberdeen and Plymouth, and from 5 to 8 April 1842 delegates from fifty-one places assembled in Birmingham under Sturge's leadership. They included not only Lovett and Collins but O'Brien, Vincent, Lowery and Gammage. O'Connor took the move seriously enough to summon a rival meeting in Birmingham at the same time. Yet it was the Sturge meeting, not his, which turned into a Chartist triumph. One by one motions in favour of the Six Points of the Charter were carried and while the name 'Charter' was not taken over, the question of whether to retain it was left to a later conference.

By the time the second conference took place on 27 December 1842, O'Connor (along with other Chartists) had made what was by now a familiar switch of tactics and had supported Sturge at a Nottingham by-election in August. More important, the country had experienced a summer of discontent, with Lancashire, the Potteries and Scotland the main centres of open violence and with the Anti-Corn Law League as well as the Chartists being blamed for bitter strikes that damaged property. Unemployment and hunger were at the heart of this outbreak, which ended with strikers returning to work on the employers' terms.

There was an aftermath. Large numbers of Chartists were imprisoned, among them Thomas Cooper, self-taught Leicester Chartist, who had been drawn into the movement when as a reporter he witnessed appalling poverty and misery in his own city and who now spent two years in a Staffordshire gaol. In that county there were no fewer than 274 trials, culminating in 154 sentences of imprisonment, and no fewer than 54 sentences of transportation. In the words of one victim, there had been 'a Tory reign of terror': on this occasion the Whigs were left out of the picture, although Tory radicals had not been silent when O'Connor had supported Sturge at the Nottingham by-election. Oastler called this O'Connor's biggest mistake.

Sturge was, in fact, routed at the December conference of the CSU, which quickly and effectively destroyed it. Attended by O'Connor as well as by representatives of all shades of Chartism, the conference stood firmly by the name of the Charter. Sturge's biographer H. Richard drew his own moral: 'Mr Sturge's friends felt thankful that this result left him at liberty honourably to withdraw from much uncongenial fellowship.' O'Connor had different problems. In 1843 he appeared in court again at Lancaster on a charge of 'seditious conspiracy', along with other members of the NCA executive, among them Harney and M'Douall. At the end of the day they were not sent to prison. 'I am sorry that Feargus [O'Connor] escaped', wrote Prince Albert to Peel.

The following year O'Connor was to engage himself in public debate with Cobden at Northampton, where M'Douall had stood as a hustings candidate in 1841. O'Connor was unconvincing, and according to the ever-critical Gammage had made matters worse by travelling to Northampton on the same train as Cobden and fraternising with him after the meeting. In 1846 he accepted repeal as a *fait accompli*. By then, however, he had moved in a new direction, following, it seemed, more in the footsteps of Cobbett than of Hunt and launching the Land Plan with which his name will always be associated. The idea of settling workers on the land in 'people's farms' was not his own – it had been anticipated, for example, in Manchester – but O'Connor generalised it and having fallen in love with his dream tried to turn it into practice by publishing with a fellow Chartist *A Practical Work on the Management of Small Farms* in 1843. He had no intention of diverting Chartists from universal suffrage. As one Chartist put it in 1845 when the Chartist Land Society was launched, 'the Land Plan was well calculated to keep up the Chartist agitation. The people wanted something tangible.'

The fact that the Land Society ultimately crashed (very soon, indeed, in 1848) does not mean that it was a failure from its inception. Yet it promised too much, as O'Connor so often did, and only about 250 people out of 70,000 were actually settled on the land. There were five settlements, the first of which, O'Connorville, echoed the name of his father's old estate in Ireland, Connerville: it was to be renamed Heronsgate, and the fate of the cottages and plots remaining there was to be one of the subjects raised (with A.J.P. Taylor as a witness) at a public enquiry on the M25 in the 1980s. Another estate at Minster Lovell in Oxfordshire, called Charterville, had recently been destroyed in favour of a modern housing estate, leaving the schoolhouse in what Taylor called 'solitary glory'.

The collapse of the Land Company in the year of revolutions was preceded by a Chartist revival, related yet again to 'distress'. After the trough of deep depression in 1842 the economy had boomed, largely on account of the ripple effects of the construction of railways. Now in 1847 the railway bubble burst, two bad harvests led to a sharp rise in the price of corn, employment fell, and Peel, who had reorganised fiscal policy, ceased to be Prime Minister, giving way again to the Whigs, this time with Russell as Prime Minister.

In this 'bad year' O'Connor, attacking 'do-nothing kid reformers', won a seat in Parliament – for Nottingham – at the general election. At the same election Harney confronted Palmerston at Tiverton, leaving a marked impression on voters and non-voters alike – and on Palmerston. O'Connor's victory provided a stimulus to renewed agitation, the prelude to 1848: there had been no branch of the NCA in Nottingham before he appeared as a candidate. There was, however, deep distress which led a local banker to conclude that 'a starving man does not discuss the principles of the party he may join. He only hopes . . . to better his condition which he believes cannot be worse.' When, months later, after Kennington Common, Chartist leaders, including M'Douall, met other local leaders in Nottingham at a meeting called by the Mayor, a local curate could still call the Charter 'the standard of discontent'.

After winning his seat O'Connor invited all old Chartists 'to return to the popular embrace and join in a national jubilee', naming specifically the characters who had represented the 'dissevered elements' of the movement, 'the O'Briens, Lovetts, Vincents, Coopers and all'. They did not. Meanwhile, O'Connell had disappeared from the scene. He died at Genoa on 15 May 1847. In 1847 and 1848 the fate of Ireland was in other hands. Some new Irish elements were pro-Chartist. They changed the political landscape in London and the north.

The events of the year 1848, including the preparation of the third National Petition, were put in perspective in the first chapter of this book. For a time London was at the very centre of the Chartist story, as it never had been before. There was no Chartist unanimity, however, as the year passed into history, with a peak in provincial Chartist activity in the summer – after Kennington Common. There were more 'dissevered elements' in Chartism after 1848 than there were when Chartism was in the making. There was still hope, but the sense of history moving round as much as moving on was plain in a speech of Ernest Jones, delivered early in 1848:

> We must agitate and organise! One simultaneous meeting, at one hour of one day all over the United Kingdom, to shew our organisation. One vast petition, to prove to the people themselves how strong they are in numbers. One vast procession of the men of London to present it, while a Convention watches the debate.

At least the vast processions continued after 10 April and there was more violence after that date than there had been before. Yet the sense that nothing had been resolved was made equally plain in a speech by Harney that followed that of Jones: 'Our Petition will be the very vanity of vanities, unless the people exhibit the will and determination to take other steps to enforce their claims.' Back to 1839.

FOUR

The Chartists

In 1848 as in 1838 there was no single Chartist type, although all Chartists attached significance to the word Charter. Each had his own profile. All Chartists would have thought of themselves, however, as 'sons of toil', bees, not drones, members of the 'industrious classes'. Magistrates representing the aristocracy and the gentry dismissed them as 'people calling themselves Chartists'. It was a deliberately patronising way of putting it. These were the missionaries, who along with journalists, were the emissaries of Chartism. But there was a different way of putting it: Chartists often referred to themselves by using a word with an old pedigree – 'patriot'.

For most of the Chartist rank and file the words 'working class' – it never was an entirely exclusive term – carried with them almost as much significance as the word 'Charter'. These were the Chartists who wore 'fustian jackets', and O'Connor, who was quite different in background (and income) from most of them, was, according to his own account, as proud of wearing such a jacket as he was of being the descendent of ancient Irish kings. At Kennington Common, however, such jackets were rare, as Francis Place would appreciate. There always was a gulf between London Chartists and the 'provincials'.

By the year 1848 there was a Chartist 'old guard', reinforced by, sometimes challenged by, new intakes, many of them younger than most of the members of the 1839 Convention. Age mattered as well as class. At Manchester the Chartists themselves called 1848 rioters 'mischievous imps and lads'; of fourteen people taken into custody only four Chartists were older than twenty.

Dr Fletcher, a surgeon representing two Lancashire 'constituencies' in 1839, recalled how in the Convention 'there were barristers, clergymen, as well as members of my own profession, and literary men [*The Northern Star* was packed with poems], and

[Fletcher's climax] a considerable proportion of honest and intelligent working men'. Harney's perspectives both in 1839 and in 1848 were quite different, but it was in the light of his experience during this decade that he suggested in 1848 that the movement should look more 'to those masses of physical force, which even at present, though deplorably wanting in mental power, strike alarm into the minds and supporters of the existing system'.

In the twilight years of Chartism Jones was less enthusiastic about such a vision than Harney. What could have been more formal than a notice that he inserted in the 'Messages' section of *The Northern Star* in 1851?

> Ernest Jones reported that he has made more arrangements for his [lecture] tour, and would commence his engagements at Exeter on Monday 4th August, by delivering two lectures. From there he should visit Torquay (two lectures), Devenport, Plymouth, Bristol, Bridgwater, Merthyr Tydvil (two lectures) . . .

There was more of a flavour of Lovett than of O'Connor in this announcement.

Recent research has shown that 'the trades' – and there was a wide range of them – played a bigger role in Chartism than was once suggested. The story is complicated both in economic and institutional terms – and the story of the role of the handloom weavers, many of whom were Chartists, is itself only superficially simple. Ballads may help. A Chartist ballad welcoming the release from prison of Lovett and Collins in 1840 grouped Birmingham Chartists poetically:

> There's colliers and miners and labourers too,
> Gun-makers, stampers and casters a few,
> All bravely united, courageous and true . . .
> There's tailors, shoemakers, and masons likewise,
> The plasterers and bricklayers strongly do rise,
> The great nobs of this town are struck with surprise.'

This was very much a Birmingham list. The profiles of localities are as distinctive as those of the Chartists. What other town but Barnsley would have renamed its May Day Green 'the Bull Ring' 'in unison with our friends in Birmingham'? Statistics, however unreliable, are sometimes available.

Sheffield issued almost twice as many NCA membership cards as Birmingham between March 1841 and October 1842, and Leicester issued more than Manchester.

It has become customary to divide Chartists, like the 'working classes' as a whole, into 'rough' and 'respectable'; and both types – and they are at best types – could be found in all communities, big and small. Temperance – or teetotalism – as the precondition of all forms of mutual and self-improvement, was often the criterion for respectability. On the reverse side of the coin the public house was a centre of social life in the 1830s and 1840s, as it has been ever since, and there were some Chartists who were publicans, just as there were some who were shopkeepers. R.J. Richardson, Manchester delegate to the Convention, had been both, and he ended life as a building surveyor. He was active in local affairs, as many Chartists were – he became a police commissioner at Salford in 1839 – and in 1854 he told a Parliamentary Committee that he had been 'personally involved in every movement that has taken place among the working classes since I can remember'.

A Lancashire Chartist of a different kind, who tired of Richardson's long and learned speeches at the Convention, was Richard Marsden, a handloom weaver, whose date and place of birth are both uncertain. He made his first political speech at the inaugural meeting of an Operative Radical Association in Preston; and he had given evidence to a Parliamentary Committee on handloom weavers before he made his remarkable speech at the Convention vividly describing the plight of his fellow workers. The industrial village near Preston from which he came was described in a London newspaper as 'one of the half civilised villages of the cotton districts'.

Lovett's vision of a more civilised as well as a more democratic society – the two for him went together – did not rest on any Christian foundation. Yet there were Chartists who were committed Christians (including not only Anglicans and Methodists but also small sects) as well as Owenite Chartists who had their own different religion and Paineites who had none. Most Chartists knew their Bible. The shortest sentence attributed to Richardson is 'The voice of the people is the voice of God'. *The Northern*

Star could claim in January 1843 that Chartism 'is superior to Christianity in this respect that it takes its name from no man . . . What greater honour can a man have than to be a Chartist?'

It is the word 'man', perhaps, that now stands out most in this extraordinary passage. In fact, women played a bigger part in the Chartist story than was once recognised. The BPU organised women's meetings before the Charter was drafted, and at the 1839 Convention Collins reported that 24,000 of the Birmingham signatures on the National Petition were those of women. In the north of England, where Richardson was another early enthusiast for women's rights, Dorothy Thompson has suggested that 'some of the steam' went out of women's protests after the decline of the movement against the New Poor Law, and that from the middle 1840s women became 'less prominent' in the Chartist story.

Changes in the workplace and changes in the family seem in part to have been responsible – as much, perhaps, as changes in Chartism itself. At the height of its appeal Chartism was a movement that involved whole families, including children, rather than individuals, and many of the children were given Chartist first names – particularly the name of Feargus – often with O'Connor attached. Looking back to the generation before, Frost called one of his sons (born in 1822) Henry Hunt Frost. It was appropriate that Frost himself inspired the names given to others. John Frost Hurst was baptised in February 1841. One Chartist family, the Waltons, chose as first names for their four children Adam Henry Vincent M'Douall, George Arthur Feargus O'Connor, John Frost and Margaret Lovett Collins. As Dorothy Thompson has remarked, 'it is to be hoped that the young Waltons showed more amity in the family circle than was shown by their namesakes in the world of politics'.

FIVE

Interpretations

The story of Chartism had no single moral, not even disunity, although there were Chartists and non-Chartists who attempted to discover and identify one. Nor were the 'lessons' that Chartists themselves felt should be taken to heart as simple as they sometimes looked. Indeed, some of the so-called lessons were contradictory. 'The leaders of the English proletarians have proved that they are true Democrats and no shams', Howard Morton, new to the ranks of the Chartists, wrote in Harney's *Red Republican* in 1850, 'by going ahead so rapidly . . . They have progressed from the idea of a simple *political reform to the idea of a Social Revolution.*'

But had they? The idea of a social revolution did not carry with it mass appeal then or at any time in the history of Chartism. Nor was it taken seriously by governments, Whig or Tory. As John Saville has written in his introduction to a modern reprint of the *Red Republican* (1966):

> There was often anxiety and unease: of that there is much evidence, but there was never any serious dent in the massive confidence of government or the propertied classes . . . throughout the whole Chartist period.

What happened at Kennington Common on 10 April 1848 in itself confirms this judgement, although the words 'massive confidence', balanced as they are against 'anxiety and unease', do not take account either of the social concern that could accompany the confidence or the doubt that could affect groups as well as individuals.

In 1840 Thomas Carlyle, fresh from writing his *French Revolution*, and looking prophetically, as always, for 'signs of the times', expressed both. Unlike Harney or Jones he was alarmed by what he witnessed, not inspired. His essay *Chartism* described it as 'delirious', 'the bitter discontent grown fierce and mad, the wrong condition, therefore, or the wrong disposition of the working classes of England.

Chartism is a new name for a thing which has had many names, which will yet have many.' It 'did not begin yesterday, will by no means end this day or tomorrow'. It was one of a number of nineteenth-century 'isms' that moved the discontented to action. Each has its own history.

Carlyle, who knew little of Chartism at first hand, sympathised with the Chartists, as did Benjamin Disraeli, the Tory politician who was to break with his leader Peel and divide his party on the issue of free trade versus protection; but he had even less confidence in Chartist aims or Chartist programmes than Disraeli had. Described by one Scottish reviewer as a preacher of 'heroic Toryism', Carlyle believed in work, not in the democratic claims of working men, and he conceived of Chartism not as a movement demanding working-class independence but as a cry for guidance from other groups in a society that as a whole had gone astray. Disraeli, not so obviously a prophet, offered a more prophetic long-term comment than Carlyle did: 'Where Wat Tyler failed, Henry Bolingbroke changed a dynasty, and although Jack Straw was hanged, a Lord John

Straw may become a Secretary of State.' The comment has topical point.

What of O'Connor's interpretation of the movement that he led as he turned back to thinking in his last years of reason about Ireland where his political life had begun. After protracted negoti-ations, his Land Plan was finally wound up in August 1851. As Chartist leaders emerged who were unwilling to follow him unreservedly, he came to appreciate the need to work more closely with 'the middle classes': he was even prepared to cooperate with Hume. He had always professed the need for 'junction' if possible, but always on his own terms. There was bound to be argument about them: his strength was that he had the platform and *The Northern Star* to support him.

He was aware, of course, of the importance of class as a rallying call. It was in Brighton, not in Oldham, that a local Chartist leader described 'the middle class', lumping many groups together, as 'a class characterised by selfishness and a want of sympathy'. 'It is not the man individually whom we denounce,' he went on, but 'the mercenary, tyrannical character of his class'. It was M'Douall, not O'Connor, who put the standard Chartist position plainly in the speech that he made on his release from prison in 1840, the speech from which the quotation at the front of this book is taken:

> He would be the last man in the world to ask the middle class to join them, although if the middle classes wished to join them he would advise such a union, always taking care . . . if they did . . . not to let them have any power in directing the movement.

The 'independence' of Chartism insulated it from other radical influences, although it did not save it from the pressures of governmental politics (it was most often a response to them) or in the north of England from the entanglements of radical Toryism and the causes that were identified with it. Nor did it save it from personal or group divisions. It was no more easy to eliminate them when Chartism was in sharp decline than it had been when it was at its height and when many Chartists spoke in unbelievably optimistic terms about its certain and, indeed, speedy success. The first historian of Chartism, Gammage, was certainly not speaking for everyone when he asked as a leading question with O'Connor in mind, 'when will Democrats learn that . . . empty boasters are their veriest foes – that they keep away thousands of sensible men by their reckless extravagances and impudent assertions?'

This interpretation of Chartist 'failure', which was accepted by Hovell, is incomplete, although it rightly raises the question, which requires fuller attention than is possible in this brief history, of why 'thousands of men' – were they all sensible? – never became Chartists. O'Connor, for all his bluster, was certainly not solely responsible for this. Indeed, he was probably more successful than any other leader would have been in maximising numbers. The numbers varied: the agitation went on. Harney, who usually had no shortage of answers, raised the same question as Gammage raised:

> It is a terrible fact', he wrote in 1849, 'that after so many years of "Reform" and "Chartist" agitation, multitudes of men whose very interest would benefit by the triumph of Chartism are as yet ignorant of or indifferent to the Charter.

This is true not only of the agricultural workers, but of a considerable portion of the local population.

To explain why demands more than brief references to 'deference' or 'apathy' or to 'religion' or 'reform'. It involves moving out of the world of myth within which O'Connor and many of his devoted followers moved into the 'real world' of early Victorian Britain, where structures and motives were mixed and where feelings were strong. Viewed in retrospect, Chartism belongs to a highly distinctive period in the political, economic and social history of Britain.

There were many prophets in the 1840s, but none (including Marx) could have foreseen how the same difficult dilemmas (tactical and moral) faced by Chartist protesters would confront popular leaders in a twentieth-century Third World not then even in the making – from South Africa to Indonesia. There may be no simple lessons in Chartism, but there is ample scope both for continuing study and for reflection.

Further Reading

There are two important bibliographies of Chartism: D. Thompson and J.F.C. Harrison, *Bibliography of the Chartist Movement* (Hassocks, 1978) and O.R. Ashton, R. Fyson and S. Roberts (eds.), *The Chartist Movement: A New Annotated Bibliography* (London, 1995).

Much of the most interesting and revealing writing on Chartism is to be found in local publications and in British, American and other historical journals. Much too has never been published. This includes university theses. A good example is 'Chartism in Brighton' (University of Sussex, PhD, 1969) by Tom Kemnitz, who went on to publish articles, including an illuminating article on the Chartist National Convention, in *Albion* (1978).

For the narrative history of Chartism – and much else – see D. Thompson, *The Chartists, Popular Politics in the Industrial Revolution* (London, 1984): it should be read alongside D. Thompson (ed.), *The Early Chartists* (London, 1971) and J.A. Epstein and D. Thompson (eds.), *The Chartist Experience* (London, 1982). Earlier accounts of the movement include R.G. Gammage, *History of the Chartist Movement* (London, 1854; reprint, New York, 1969); M. Hovell, *The Chartist Movement* (Manchester, 1925 edn.); T. Rothstein, *From Chartism to*

Labourism (London, 1929; reprint, 1983); R. Graves, *But We Shall Rise Again, a Narrative History of Chartism* (London, 1938); J.T. Ward, *Chartism* (London, 1973); D.J.V. Jones, *Chartism and the Chartists* (London, 1975); and E. Royle, *Chartism* (London, 1980).

Following the publication of A. Briggs (ed.), *Chartist Studies* (London, 1959) several local studies of Chartism were published in book or pamphlet form, among them P. Searby, *Coventry Politics in the Age of the Chartists* (Coventry, 1965); P. Wyncoll, *Nottingham Chartism* (Nottingham, 1966); J. Cannon, *Chartism in Bristol* (Bristol, 1967); A.J. Peacock, *Chartism in Bradford, 1838–40* (York, 1969); S. Pollard and C. Holmes (eds.), *Essays in the Economic and Social History of South Yorkshire* (Sheffield, 1976); L. Prothero, *Artisans and Politics in Early Nineteenth Century London* (London, 1979); E.J. King, *Richard Marsden and the Preston Chartists* (Lancaster, 1982); D. Goodway, *London Chartism, 1838–48* (Cambridge, 1982); and P.A. Pickering, *Chartism and the Chartists in Manchester and Salford* (Manchester, 1995). For Scotland see A. Wilson, *The Chartist Movement in Scotland* (Manchester, 1970).

A most stimulating – and controversial – general essay on 'Rethinking Chartism' by G. Stedman Jones was included in his book *Languages of Class* (Cambridge, 1983). See also P. Joyce, *Work, Society and Politics* (Brighton, 1980) and *Visions of the People: Industrial England and the Question of Class, 1848–1914* (Cambridge, 1991).

Index

INDEX

French Revolution 18, 34, 53–4, 61
Frost, John 77–8, 100

Gaitskell, Hugh 4
Gammage, R.G. 1, 16, 20, 85, 88, 105–6
general elections 42–3, 82
Gladstone, William Ewart 6, 16, 22
Glasgow 47, 49, 60, 61

Hammond, J.L. and Barbara 21
handloom weavers 56, 96, 98
Harney, George Julian 18, 53–4, 74, 87–8, 90, 92, 95, 101, 106–7
Hartwell, Robert 41
Heronsgate 89
Hetherington, Henry 28, 35–6, 40, 85
Heywood, Abel 82
Hobson, Joshua 27
Holberry, Samuel 79–80
Horne, Joseph 34
Hovell, Mark 4, 5, 6–7, 18, 106
Hume, Joseph 34, 42, 104
Hunt, Henry 20, 38, 55

imprisonment 28–9, 74–5, 86–7
Ireland 9, 14, 22–3, 26–7, 55, 78, 104

Jones, Ernest 17–18, 92, 95

Kennington Common (10 April 1848) 13–14, 21–2, 91–2, 94, 102

Labour Party 1–2, 4, 5, 6, 23
Lancashire 11, 44, 45, 47, 48, 86, 98
land plans 12–13, 18, 88–9, 104
Land Society 89
Leeds 41, 84
Leicester 86–7, 97
Lenin 7
Liberal Party 6, 15, 17
London 46–7, 91
  see also Crown and Anchor;
  Kennington Common
London Working Men's Association

(LWMA) 8, 35–7, 42–5, 48, 55, 58–9, 60
Lovelace, George 64
Lovett, William 8, 24, 25–6, 27, 35–6, 43, 98
  imprisoned 73, 75, 81
  and O'Connor 30–1, 32, 66, 82
  quoted 49–50, 85
Lowery, Robert 17, 85

Macaulay, T.B. 16
Malthusianism 32–3
Manchester 52, 71, 81, 82, 88, 94, 97, 107
Marsden, Richard 98
Marx, Karl 6, 81
Matthews, Robin 10
Mayne, Richard 13–14
M'Douall, Peter Murray 72, 75, 80, 82, 88, 91, 105
Melbourne, Lord 61–2, 68
Morton, Howard 101

Napier, Sir Charles 70–1, 74
National Charter Association 31, 81–2, 83–4, 90, 96–7
National Union of Working Classes 28
Newcastle-upon-Tyne 45, 50, 52, 79
Newport Rising 77–9
North of England 26, 41, 47, 50, 105
Northern Liberator 45, 61, 76
Northern Star 26–7, 30–1, 39–40, 74, 94, 95, 98–9, 104
Nottingham 38, 56, 70, 86, 87, 90, 91

Oastler, Richard 28, 32–3, 36, 55, 70
O'Brien, Bronterre 8–9, 11–12, 23, 28, 36, 41–2, 53, 64, 82, 85
O'Connell, Daniel 9, 31–2, 55–6, 91
O'Connor, Feargus 4, 8, 106
  death 15
  disputes 30–2, 82
  imprisoned 28–9, 31–2, 74
  Land Plan 88–9, 104

INDEX